People of the   New Testament

a glimpse into the world of
Jesus' first followers

Caroline Fletcher

Published by Redemptorist Publications
Wolf's Lane, Chawton, Hampshire, GU34 3HQ, UK
Tel. +44 (0)1420 88222. Fax. +44 (0)1420 88805
Email customercare@rpbooks.co.uk, www.rpbooks.co.uk

A registered charity limited by guarantee
Registered in England 03261721

First published June 2024

Edited by Caroline Hodgson
Designed by Jeni Child

ISBN 978-0-85231-641-2

A CIP catalogue record for this book is available from the British Library.

The publisher gratefully acknowledges permission to use the following
copyright material:

Excerpts from the New Revised Standard Version of the Bible: Anglicised Edition,
© 1989, 1995, Division of Christian Education of the National Council of
the Churches of Christ in the United States of America. Used by permission.
All rights reserved.

Printed by Bishops Printers Ltd.,
Walton Rd, Drayton, Portsmouth PO6 1TR

Contents

About the author

Caroline Fletcher came to faith through studying the Bible at A level and her love of the Bible sent her on to study biblical studies at Sheffield University. In later years she returned for further study and completed a Master of Philosophy that delved into church history as well as scripture. She has worked in schools as a RE teacher and a literacy tutor, as well as working as an open-learning tutor for a number of Bible colleges.

Caroline has lived all over the UK but is currently in Chesterfield near the beautiful Peak District. She works as a freelance writer, regularly producing devotional work for Christian publishers such as Scripture Union, the Bible Reading Fellowship and Redemptorist Publications.

To my husband, Tim,
for your support and feedback
in the writing of this book

"An insightful and user-friendly study guide written with warmth and thoughtfulness. A useful tool for individuals and study groups which should prompt conversation and debate."

The Reverend Kate Bottley

"People of the New Testament shines a spotlight on the characters who have minor roles in the Bible but who have a great deal to teach us. Caroline Fletcher's clear and lively studies will introduce the reader to fresh insights and build faith, hope and love through a deeper reading of scripture."

+Steven Croft, Bishop of Oxford

Foreword

by +Sophie Jelley, Bishop of Doncaster

As one who has spent much of my life encouraging people to grow in their knowledge and love of God through engagement with the Bible and taking their place in the company of Jesus' followers through the Church, this book is a delight. It offers a beautiful introduction to some of the earliest followers of Jesus, whose names are recorded in the New Testament but about whom we may have little knowledge. In their own way, each of these were friends and supporters along "the way", the name for those who followed Jesus in New Testament times. There is no doubt that it remains challenging to follow Jesus today and that we can gain much from deepening our knowledge and being inspired by the saints who have gone before.

Caroline has chosen her saints carefully. Her love of scripture and passion for learning are evident throughout. Reading her work feels a bit like being led by a wise and knowledgeable tour guide, through a place you thought you knew reasonably well, but whose insight enables fascinating discoveries.

The author is one who has lived with and loves the Bible, still. From her rich background of scholarship, teaching and the devotional application of scripture, she is well placed to bring these characters to life. We are offered a biographical and historical context for each, alongside a careful reading of the biblical text. Caroline has made discerning choices based on her understanding of the material, which those wanting to go deeper can explore from the endnotes provided. What is most heartening about the book is that it leads us to an appreciation of the vocational aspect of these recorded lives, as we see the part each played in the unfolding narrative of the early Church. Inspirational in itself, and also motivational, in that it presents us with an all-important question: what is my part in the continuing narrative of God's Church today?

I believe it is this that makes the book as relevant for the new believer as for the seasoned disciple, and hopefully as helpful for the Sunday-school teacher as for the Bible-college student. Each could be equally refreshed and challenged by it. It would also be a useful text to take on retreat, dwelling with a character at a time, and seeing through their eyes as they played their part in God's story. From years of working with people who are trying to discern the call of God in their lives, these often simple yet profound examples of "ordinary" people, responding to the invitation of God through Jesus, can remind us all that we are called to walk by faith into the unknown, trusting that God is faithful.

You will no doubt be familiar with the saying "It takes a village to raise a child." I often reflect on the fact that it takes a church to raise a disciple. To follow Jesus has always been a challenging if rewarding path and we all need friends and supporters along the way. I trust that in reading this book you will discover new friends and supporters or, at least, new insights about them as you delve into their stories of faith and hopefully deepen your own.

+Sophie Jelley, Bishop of Doncaster, February 2024

Introduction

I first started researching some of these lesser-known New
Testament characters when I was writing a series of small
pieces for Redemptorist Publications' *Sunday Link*. People
like Priscilla, Barnabas and Onesimus are only mentioned
briefly in the Bible, so I figured they would be perfect subjects
for a few 150-word articles. However, 150 words turned out
to be far from enough – there was so much more that could
be said about every one of them. I quickly realised that each
character shows us something unique about that fascinating
period of time when Jesus walked the earth and the first
churches were established.

Many people today find it hard to read the Bible. Centuries have
come and gone since the books of the New Testament were first
written and the world it portrays can be hard for us to relate to
and understand, as it is so very different from our own. Yet buried
within its pages are real-life, fallible characters just like you and
me – people who actually knew and spent time with Jesus,
who lived and laboured alongside Peter and Paul and the other
apostles. Learning about these people provides us with a way
into that world, a window on it, and reveals more about subjects
such as the mindset of the Pharisees; how Israel was governed;
Christianity's Jewish roots; the radical attitudes of Jesus and so
much more.

The characters described in my book, characters such as
Barnabas and John Mark, do not leap out of the Bible on first
reading, as Paul or Peter do. They receive only fleeting mentions
in a few verses scattered across the pages of the New Testament.
But these people were vitally important. Without Barnabas,
for instance, Paul would not have been given the chance

to become a missionary, and without John Mark so many stories about Jesus, stories that may well have come from Peter himself, would never have been recorded and passed down to us. Indeed, every one of the characters in this book played an important role in the development of Christianity in their own way. I hope, then, as you read through these chapters, these individuals and the world they inhabited really come to life for you, and you are left with an increased understanding of and interest in the Bible.

Of course, because we only have limited details about these characters, there is some speculation involved when putting together their stories and I have often had to decide between different scholarly views. In this I am grateful for the work of the many biblical theologians I have referenced in this book. I have sought not to complicate the text too much by going into differing arguments and alternative possibilities in huge detail, but for those who are interested, the endnotes show where I have drawn ideas from and offer a way to investigate these characters further.

I also hope that learning more about the lives of these people will be an encouragement to us all in one further way. I hope it will remind us that each of us has an important part to play, even if we are not big characters with upfront roles. Paul may have been a ground-breaking missionary and leader, but he needed the help of faithful co-workers like Luke, Priscilla and Timothy, while Jesus valued the friendship and practical support of Mary of Bethany and Joanna. None of us works in isolation. We are all part of the body of Christ, just as these Christian brothers and sisters before us and, like them, we all have vital roles to play.

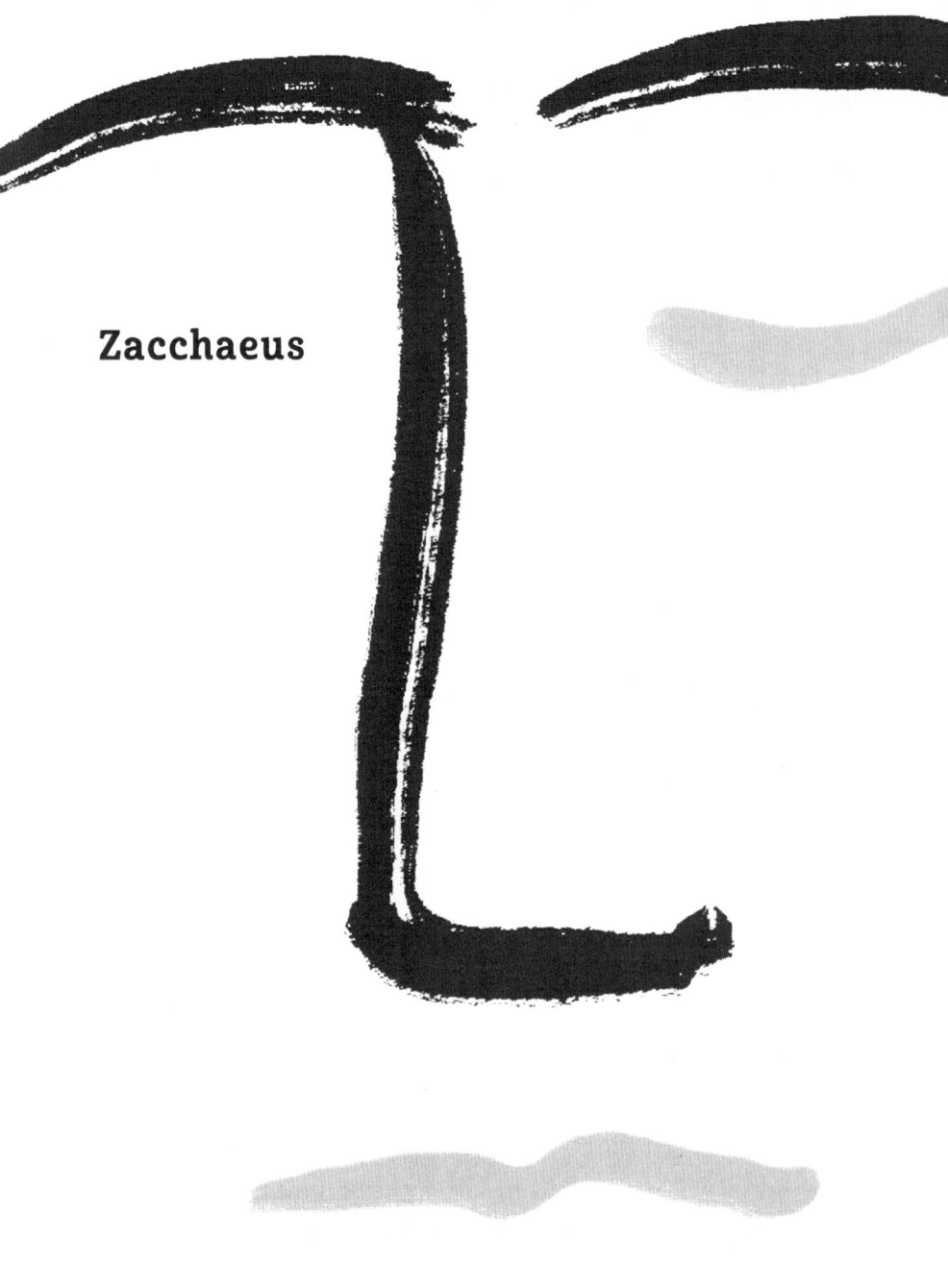

Zacchaeus

Zacchaeus

(Luke 19:1-10)

The story of Zacchaeus' meeting with Jesus will be familiar to many people from Sunday school. It's a popular tale to tell children and it's easy to see why. Poor Zacchaeus was too short to see Jesus over the crowd, a situation that small children readily relate to. The tale has a comedy factor, too: kids love to see adults in embarrassing situations and here we have the amusing image of a wealthy man hitching up his rich robes and clambering up a tree in a most undignified manner to catch a glimpse of Christ.

However, there is a deeper message behind this story. Modern readers may not pick up just how controversial Jesus' friendship with this man was. It's possible to read the first six verses of the story in Luke 19 without seeing it as anything more than a funny little tale. Verse 7, however, makes it clear that there was no affection for Zacchaeus among the people of Jericho. They did not mince their words about him. In their eyes he was "a sinner". Zacchaeus was despised, and the people of Jericho were horrified to see Jesus with him.

What, then, had Zacchaeus done to cause everyone to dislike him so? The answer was that he was a tax collector. Of course, even today tax collectors are rarely popular, but we may well be shocked by the extent of the crowd's hatred for this man.

It was normal at the time for this profession to be rejected and ostracised. Tax collectors were banned from worshipping in synagogues and were associated in people's minds with robbers and murderers.[1] They were not allowed to be judges or even to act as witnesses in trials, effectively denying them the rights normally granted to Israelites and putting them on a par with Gentile slaves.[2]

People of Jesus' day were expected to pay a number of different taxes. The tax collectors mentioned in the New Testament collected tolls and duties. They would have been stationed at booths set up on main roads, at ports and the entrances to cities. Jesus' disciple Matthew, for instance, was sitting at his tax booth when he was called (Matthew 9:9). Jericho, where Zacchaeus worked, was a big commercial centre which lay on an important trade route, providing many opportunities for customs to be collected. Tax collectors could force people to unpack their baggage to show them the goods they had purchased, so they could charge taxes on these, and they would also charge tolls for using roads, ports and markets, even charging people for their carts and the animals that pulled them.[3] Another reason why the Jewish tax collectors were disliked by their fellow countrymen was because they collected taxes on behalf of the Romans, leading them to be seen as traitors. However, it was their reputation for corruption that was the main cause of their unpopularity. They had paid money upfront to the Romans for the right to collect taxes, and made their profit by raising more money from collecting taxes than they paid to the Romans. The system was open to abuse, and the temptation for many was to increase their profits as much as possible by demanding far higher duties on goods than they were supposed to. No wonder the New Testament lumped them together with sinners, robbers and prostitutes, and ordinary people considered them no better than common thieves.

The Jews in Jesus' day, living under Roman rule, were taxed in numerous ways. As well as the tolls and duties demanded by collectors such as Zacchaeus, they were forced to pay other, heavy taxes on land and crops. Not only that, but there were religious taxes to pay to the Jewish leaders for the upkeep and running of the Temple. For people who owned land, like farmers, these taxes on land and crops together with the Temple tax came to a massive thirty-five per cent of their income, so to impose heavy tolls and duties on top of this would be totally unbearable. No wonder men like Zacchaeus were so unpopular!

This reputation for corruption is reflected in John the Baptist's words to the tax collectors who came to hear him preach: "Collect no more than the amount prescribed for you" (Luke 3:12-13). Jesus, too, was aware how deeply unpopular these men were, even though he chose to mix with them. In terms of reputation, they were probably on a par with modern-day drug dealers. (See also Matthew 18:17; 21:31, Mark 2:15, Luke 18:11.)

How incredible, then, that Jesus sought out, socialised with and befriended tax collectors, especially one like Zacchaeus who, as a chief tax collector, is likely to have been particularly corrupt to have risen to that position. As Michael Card writes, "Zacchaeus is not misunderstood. He is not the victim of circumstance. He is a genuinely bad man".4 And Zacchaeus was not the only tax collector whom Jesus associated with. He even called one to be one of his disciples! At Jesus' request Matthew (also known as Levi) left his tax booth to become one of the Twelve. One wonders how the other disciples reacted to Matthew's inclusion in their group, especially the one known as Simon the Zealot. If he had strong anti-Roman feelings as some think the word "zealot" suggests, it must have been extremely difficult for him to get on with Matthew, who had made a living collaborating with Rome.

Jesus' friendships with tax collectors often involved going
to their homes and sharing meals with them. He did this
with Matthew and his fellow tax collectors (Matthew 9:10)
and he would also have shared a meal with Zacchaeus, for
we are told he stayed at his house. It was this habit, of sharing
meals with tax collectors and others whom society viewed as
sinners, that offended people the most. This was probably what
lay behind the criticism that Jesus was "a glutton and a drunkard,
a friend of tax collectors and sinners" (11:19). We can see such
disapproval in how the crowd responded to Jesus going to
Zacchaeus' house: "All who saw it began to grumble and said,
'He has gone to be the guest of one who is a sinner'" (Luke 19:7).
Similarly, when the Pharisees saw him share a meal with
Matthew and other tax collectors, they asked his disciples,
"Why does your teacher eat with tax collectors and sinners?"
(Matthew 9:11).

Why was eating with such people offensive to so many?
Because Palestine was occupied by the Romans, many
Jews were worried that they would lose their identity and
become indistinguishable from Gentiles. They wanted to retain
their distinctiveness as a nation, central to which was living up
to the requirements expected of a people set apart and chosen
by God. They knew their history: the scriptures reminded them
how God had punished their ancestors for forgetting the Lord
and taking on board the thinking of pagan peoples around them.
Although their exile in Babylon had happened hundreds of
years before, it remained a powerful reminder of the retribution
they could face for forgetting God and turning to Gentile ways.
They wanted to be free of their Roman oppressors and believed
that separating themselves out from sinful influences would
purify Israel, please God and encourage the Lord to deliver
them from their enemies.

This meant that adhering to their religious laws and avoiding bad influences became especially important to Jews such as the Pharisees, who took their faith extremely seriously. Refusing to share meals with sinners (those who did not keep the religious laws or whose occupations were considered incompatible with the faith) was thought vital in avoiding the corrupting effect of such people. The mantra of the Pharisees was Leviticus 19:2: "You shall be holy, for I the Lord your God am holy," and being holy involved keeping away from bad influences.

However, there was possibly an even more important reason for avoiding eating with sinners. Eating together was a sign of fellowship and fraternity. This meant meals had a symbolic meaning too. Not only did your dinner guests reflect who you got on with and liked, but they revealed who you thought was acceptable to God. The Pharisees wanted to cleanse Israel and make it holy and the likes of tax collectors and other flagrant wrongdoers were, in their eyes, a source of contamination. Therefore they could never be in fellowship with such people and partake in the bond of a meal with them. In addition, to share dinner with someone like Zacchaeus would mean eating food he had sourced from overcharging and exploiting others, and this would be viewed as profiting from his greed and sharing in his guilt.

So why did Jesus eat with tax collectors and sinners, when he knew it was so offensive to all who were earnest about purifying Israel? When the Pharisees asked just this question, Jesus famously answered, "Those who are well have no need of a physician, but those who are sick... I have come to call not the righteous but sinners" (Matthew 9:12-13).

Sharing meals was a deliberate and provocative prophetic act on Jesus' part, powerfully challenging the common view that sinners such as tax collectors were beyond the pale. Rather than fearing that such people would contaminate him with their sin and shunning them as other religious leaders did, Jesus' controversial actions suggest that he believed that holiness was "contagious":5 that the gracious mercy of God has the power to touch even the most hardened sinners and bring them to repentance. Jesus powerfully demonstrated this gracious nature of God's love not only in his meals with sinners, but throughout his teaching. For instance, in the parable of the prodigal son, Jesus presents God as a father pining for his rebellious child to return. Day after day he keeps watch on the horizon, desperately hoping to see his son on his way home. When, finally, that longed-for day comes and he sees him from afar, the father runs to him and throws his arms about him. He does not insist that this renegade proves he has really changed before accepting him, but welcomes him home with joy. The father's love is unconditional. By eating with people like Zacchaeus, Jesus was, then, proclaiming and demonstrating God's mercy and forgiveness, making it known that no one is beyond God's grace.

This does not mean that Jesus was unconcerned about sinful behaviour, but that God's extravagant love for all has the power to move and inspire sinners to change their ways far more effectively than pronouncements of judgement and condemnation. Indeed, Jesus' act of forgiveness and grace seems to have worked dramatically in Zacchaeus' case. The rejection and criticism he experienced in his home town never motivated him to change. However, Jesus' act of acceptance and friendship touched him so much that not only did he repent but he also promised to make restitution far beyond what was required by religious law. The law demanded that he repay what he had taken plus a fifth (Leviticus 6:1-5), whereas Zacchaeus promised to repay four times the amount he had embezzled. He also said he would give away half of his possessions to the poor and, although that may not seem that much for a rich man, we should remember that his remaining wealth would be needed to repay those he had wronged.

Luke's original readers would have been shocked at Zacchaeus' wholehearted repentance and their surprise must have been heightened by how his response contrasted with that of the rich man described in the previous chapter of Luke's Gospel (verses 18-25). Unlike Zacchaeus, this rich young ruler appears to have been a good man, but when Christ told him to give away all his wealth and follow him, he could not do as Zacchaeus had done and leave behind his riches. Surprisingly, it seems the outcasts of society found it easier to follow Christ than those who were upright. As Christ himself taught, those who, like Zacchaeus, have been forgiven much, love God much (see Luke 7:36-50). This lies behind Jesus' shocking words to the chief priests and religious elders: "Truly I tell you, the tax collectors and the prostitutes are going into the kingdom of God ahead of you" (Matthew 21:31). No wonder Christ was unpopular with the religious hierarchy.

There is no reliable information on what happened to Zacchaeus after his dramatic turnaround. The second-century theologian Clement of Alexandria identified him with Matthias, the man who replaced Judas Iscariot as one of the twelve apostles. *The Clementine Homilies*, which date from around the fourth century, put forward another belief that he worked alongside Peter and became Bishop of Caesarea. The truth is we do not know. There is similar uncertainty about the fate of the sycamore fig tree that Zacchaeus climbed. Of course, by now it would be over two thousand years old and unlikely still to be standing, but there is a tree in the gardens of the Russian Museum in Jericho which draws tourists from around the world because of the belief that it is Zacchaeus' tree. However, a Greek Orthodox monastery in Jericho displays a tree trunk in a glass case which is also claimed to be the original sycamore.

Even though we know so little about Zacchaeus, his story remains as deeply moving and relevant today as when it was first written. To his contemporaries Zacchaeus was an outcast: despised, rejected and beyond all hope. To Jesus he was a precious child: loved, valued and forgiven, despite the terrible things he had done. Christ's unconditional love melted this man's heart and turned him completely around. And all these centuries later, Christ's love continues to overwhelm and transform the unlikeliest of people, no matter who they are and what they have done.

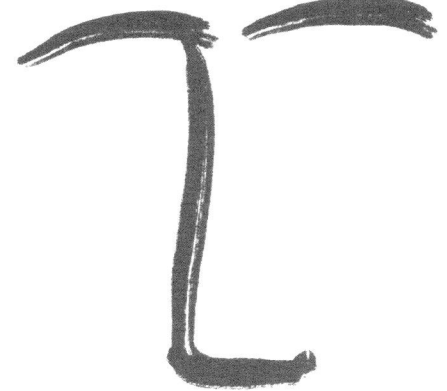

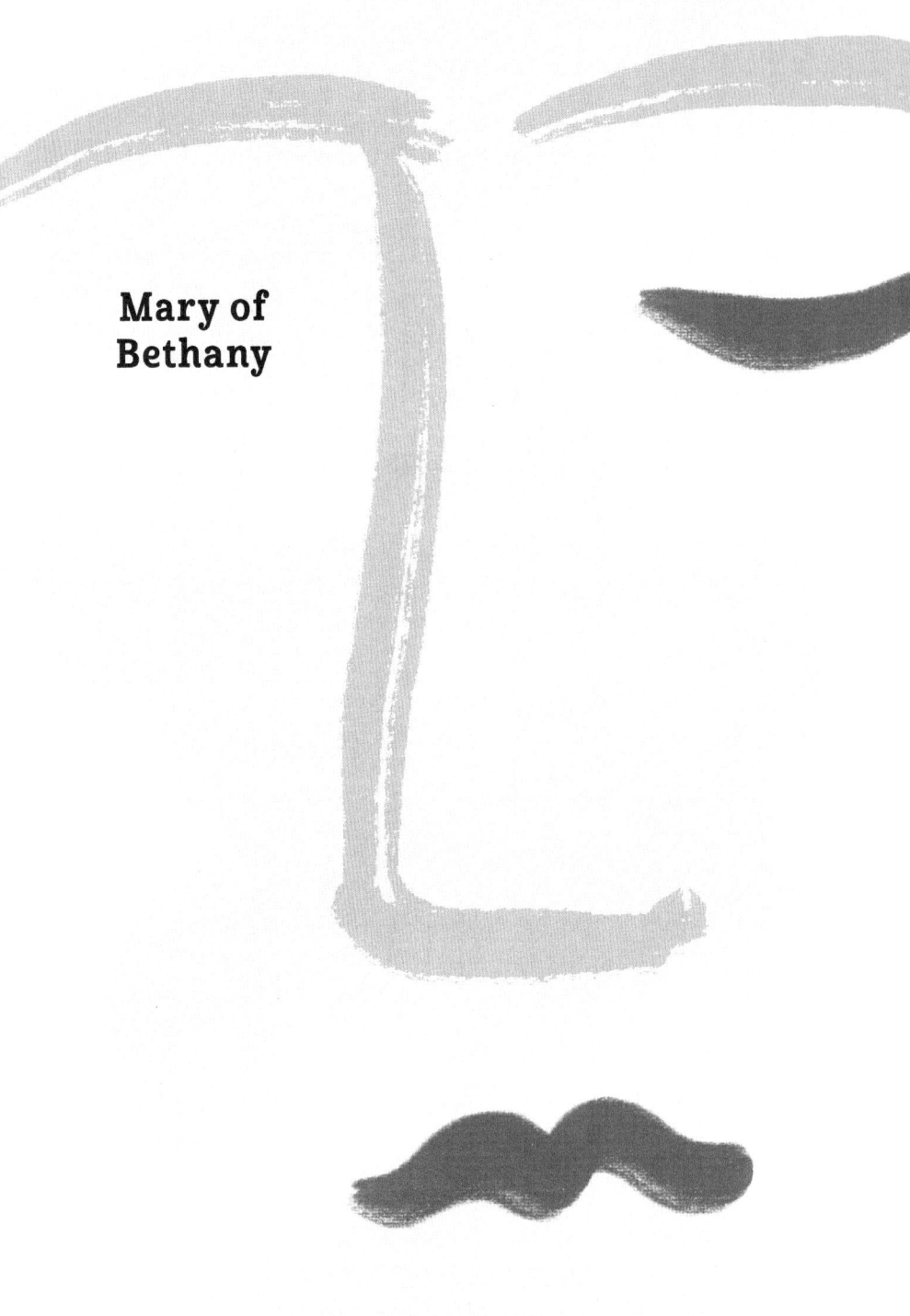

Mary of
Bethany

Mary of Bethany

(Luke 10:38-42)

Mary of Bethany is often overlooked. Sermons generally remember her for annoying her sister, Martha, by sitting at Jesus' feet and listening to him teach rather than helping her prepare the meal. But there is far more to Mary's story. She was involved in some very momentous events. She witnessed Jesus raise her brother Lazarus from the dead after he had been in the grave four whole days. She also anointed Jesus, an act of far more significance than is often realised. Even her apparent spat with Martha reveals fascinating things about the first women to follow Christ.

The story in Luke's Gospel, of Martha's frustration with Mary, is a difficult passage. As it is commonly understood, an angry Martha presses Jesus to tell Mary to give her a hand with the meal she is preparing. Christ, though, appears to have little sympathy for Martha, telling her that Mary has done the right thing by listening to him.

Many people feel uncomfortable with this take on the passage. It is odd that Jesus would fail to appreciate Martha's hard work, when he so often spoke about the importance of serving others. It also seems impractical: if Martha had been sitting at Jesus' feet too, rather than preparing the food, they would have gone hungry. Scholars have revisited this story in recent years, arguing that it is far more than a simple tale of sibling rivalry or a petty disagreement over women's work.

One of the scholars who have looked at this passage afresh is Ben Witherington III. He highlights the importance of a phrase found in verse 39: Mary "sat at the Lord's feet". Witherington explains that sitting at a teacher's feet was the normal stance for a disciple of a rabbi (a teacher) and describes this phrase as "a technical formula" indicating that Mary was a disciple of Jesus.[6] These words, then, do not necessarily show that Mary was literally sitting at Christ's feet, any more than the phrase "the footballer has been on the bench all season" means a player has been occupying a wooden pew for months.

This interpretation reveals a Mary who did not simply sit around listening to Jesus' stories but was an active disciple, learning from Christ and following him. We tend to associate the word "disciple" with the twelve apostles, men like Peter and John. However, the word is used more widely in the Bible to describe other followers of Jesus too. Some of these, like the twelve apostles, left their homes and families to follow Christ. Others, like Joseph of Arimathea, are described as disciples even though they do not appear to have travelled with him (Matthew 27:57). A fundamental part of being a disciple was learning from a teacher. In Jesus' day rabbis generally did not teach women and, by going into Mary and Martha's house, Jesus went far beyond convention. A close reading of the passage suggests that he entered their home by himself, without any of the twelve apostles. In addition, it's possible that this was a female-only household, as the passage does not mention that the sisters were living with Lazarus at this point. All of this is significant, because it suggests that Jesus was not simply allowing women to overhear the teaching he gave to men, but actively choosing to teach women in their own right. Entering a woman's home to teach her was something rabbis do not seem to have done and it would have been particularly frowned upon for a rabbi to go alone into the house of a woman he was not related to.[7] Clearly Jesus was so concerned that Mary and Martha learnt from him and he viewed it so worthwhile that he was prepared to flout convention and risk his reputation in order to pass on his wisdom to these women.

Mary Stromer Hanson, in her book *The New Perspective on Mary and Martha*, agrees with Witherington's view that the phrase "sat at Jesus' feet" indicates that Mary was a disciple, and she takes it a stage further. She argues that Mary was not even at home when Martha was talking about her to Jesus, but was, in fact, away doing Christ's work and that she was a disciple who may well have travelled around with Christ and been active in ministry herself. This is not as unlikely as it may seem, for the Bible tells us that Jesus had many female followers who accompanied him on his journeys (Luke 8:1-3). Stromer believes it was Mary's absence that lay at the heart of Martha's anxiety: she was worried about her sister far away from home, as well as missing her help. Jesus did not devalue Martha's service or view it as less spiritual than Mary's work. He simply made it clear to Martha that Mary's choice of ministry was a good one despite the worry it caused Martha.[8]

Not everyone will agree with this interpretation, but there are hints in other places that Mary of Bethany played a significant role among the first Christians. As well as the Luke passage we have already looked at, she appears in chapters 11-12 of John. Here we learn that she is Lazarus' sister or, to be more precise, that Lazarus is "her brother" (John 11:2). We are also told that he came from "Bethany, the village of Mary and her sister Martha" (verse 1). In an age where women were lower in status than men, it is significant that Lazarus is introduced to the reader through his connection with his sisters, which suggests they were better known than he was. This is even more remarkable when one considers that Lazarus was raised from the dead – an event related in chapter 11. Surely that would make him a well-known figure in his own right.

Furthermore, John 11:2 has a fascinating aside. This is the first time the fourth Gospel mentions Mary and it introduces her as "the one who anointed the Lord with perfume". We get to read about this anointing in the next chapter, but to mention it beforehand implies that the first readers of this Gospel were already familiar with Mary's act and she was well known among early Christians.

The anointing described in John 12:1-8 took place during a meal that Jesus shared with Mary, Martha and Lazarus. The perfume Mary used was called nard and it was extremely expensive: nard comes from the spikenard plant and is not native to Israel. It would have been sourced from as far away as India or the Himalayas, so the pound of nard that Mary used was worth a year's wages. It was not unusual to honour guests by anointing their head with perfumed oil, but this was sheer extravagance, an expression of Mary's overflowing love for Jesus – a love, no doubt, intensified by how grateful she was to him for restoring Lazarus to life.

Yet there was more to Mary's anointing than her immense gratitude. In John's version, Mary anoints Jesus' feet. This was not a normal part of social etiquette, but a ritual associated with preparing a body for burial. In the light of this, it could be viewed as a prophetic act, one that prepared Christ for his imminent death.[9] Mary, though, may have been fully aware of

the significance of her anointing, for there is good reason
to think she would have realised that Jesus' life was in danger.
She must have heard about the rising tension surrounding
Christ. The disciples were certainly picking up on it. When
they discovered that Jesus was going to visit the ailing
Lazarus just outside Jerusalem, they said, "the Jews were just
now trying to stone you, and are you going there again?"
(John 11:8). In addition, Jesus had told his followers on a
number of occasions that he would be put to death. Had
Mary heard Jesus say this herself and had she managed to
process this shocking information better than the twelve
apostles, who seemed unprepared for his death despite his
many warnings? (In Matthew 16:21-23, for instance, Peter
even rebuked Jesus when he told them he would be killed.)

John's Gospel is not the only account of an anointing.
All four Gospels contain stories of a woman anointing
Jesus (Matthew 26:6-13; Mark 14:3-9; Luke 7:36-50). One
of the main differences is that the other Gospels do not
name the woman, so scholars disagree as to whether these
passages refer to Mary of Bethany, or whether they describe
a separate anointing by another woman. Most believe that
the accounts in Mark and Matthew refer to the same anointing
as that recorded in John's Gospel. If so, they must also describe
Mary of Bethany. This, then, raises an interesting question.
Why would Mark and Matthew not name Mary when John's
Gospel does? This is especially curious when, according to
Mark, Jesus declared afterwards: "I tell you, wherever the good
news is proclaimed in the whole world, what she has done
will be told in remembrance of her" (Mark 14:9).

The scholar Richard Bauckham offers an interesting explanation.
Mark and Matthew are believed to have been written before
John's Gospel. He argues that the earlier Gospels kept Mary

anonymous because she was in danger from the same religious authorities that crucified Jesus. This was because her act of anointing had a further prophetic dimension beyond the one already mentioned: anointing was performed when a monarch was appointed and so she was emulating prophets such as Samuel who anointed both Saul and David as kings. She was effectively declaring Jesus to be the king the Jews had been waiting for, their Messiah.[10] If her anointing was indeed taken this way, then it would have set her on a direct collision course with the Jewish authorities.

Even if this was not how it was seen, it is still likely that her life was in danger simply because she was so close to Christ and was related to Lazarus. John's Gospel makes it very clear that, after Lazarus was raised from the dead, tension between Christ and the religious authorities spiralled, threatening not only Jesus' life but Lazarus' too (John 12:9-11). Being Lazarus' sister and a witness to the raising of her brother, the authorities are likely to have wanted to silence Mary as well. By the time John's Gospel was written, Mary would probably have died and so there would no longer have been a need to hide her identity. John could declare to all what she had done for Christ, and Mary's name could, at last, be remembered as Jesus said it would.

There is less agreement over how Luke's account (7:36-50) relates to the anointings in the other three Gospels, however. This is because it is set at a different point in Jesus' ministry; earlier during his time in Galilee, which was approximately seventy miles from Bethany, where the other accounts are set. Also, the woman in Luke is referred to as having led "a sinful life" and her story appears to be primarily about her gratitude for Christ's forgiveness.

While some people believe this is simply a different version of the event that is described in the other Gospels, many think that Luke's account refers to another event: either an anointing performed by a completely different woman, or an earlier anointing carried out by Mary of Bethany, which would mean that she actually anointed Jesus on two separate occasions.

If Mary of Bethany was, indeed, the same person as this "sinner", does that mean she must have been a prostitute, as is often assumed? Not necessarily, because the term "sinner" had a wide range of meanings in those days, including someone who did not keep the religious laws, a criminal of some sort or even simply a person who had an undesirable occupation such as a fruit seller or swineherd.[11] Frustratingly, we can only speculate about Mary's past, for we cannot be sure whether Luke's account offers us any useful insight about her or whether it describes an entirely different woman.

While much about Mary of Bethany remains a mystery, there is enough in what we have seen so far to indicate that she was a significant figure among the first Christians. Indeed, the pages of the New Testament contain more information about her than most of the twelve apostles. Despite this, in the centuries that followed, Mary of Bethany faded from view. Her unique identity was lost. From at least the sixth century the Western Church taught that she was the same person as another Mary in the Bible – Mary Magdalene. Some think this happened because of a tendency for characters with the same name to become confused over time. Others think it had more to do with the Church's negative attitude towards women which led to their contribution to early Christianity being undervalued and one woman being viewed as pretty much the same as another.

U nfortunately, we know little about what happened to
Mary of Bethany after the events recorded in the Bible.
There is a tale written by a thirteenth-century friar called
The Golden Legend, which claims to describe her life but is
so fanciful that there is little to be gleaned from it historically.
As was the custom by then, the author assumed that Mary
was Mary Magdalene. The *Legend* tells of Mary, together
with Martha and Lazarus, being forced to leave their homeland.
Antagonistic Jews threw them on to a boat which had no
means to steer it, hoping they would drown. However, the
story describes God miraculously guiding the group to France
where, among other adventures, Martha fought a dragon and
Mary ended up living as a hermit for thirty years in a cave
near Marseilles. During this time, we are told, Mary ate nothing
and was lifted up to heaven seven times a day by angels.[12]

In contrast, Orthodox tradition has Mary, Martha and Lazarus
travelling in a leaky boat to Cyprus rather than France. Here, it is
claimed, Lazarus became Bishop of Kition, modern-day Larnaca.[13]

I t is a shame that we do not know more about Mary's later
years, for as Ben Witherington says she may well have been
"the most important and prominent [woman] in Jesus' life
after His own mother".[14] However, she lives on in the pages
of the Bible for those willing to find her: a devoted disciple,
an anointing prophet and one of Christ's closest friends.

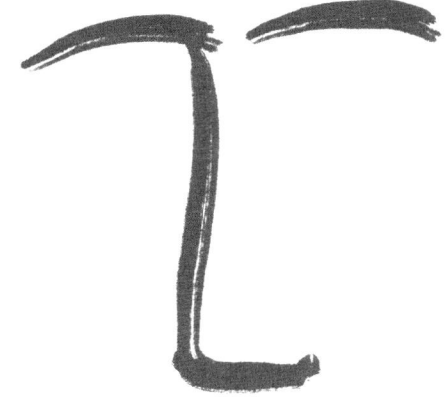

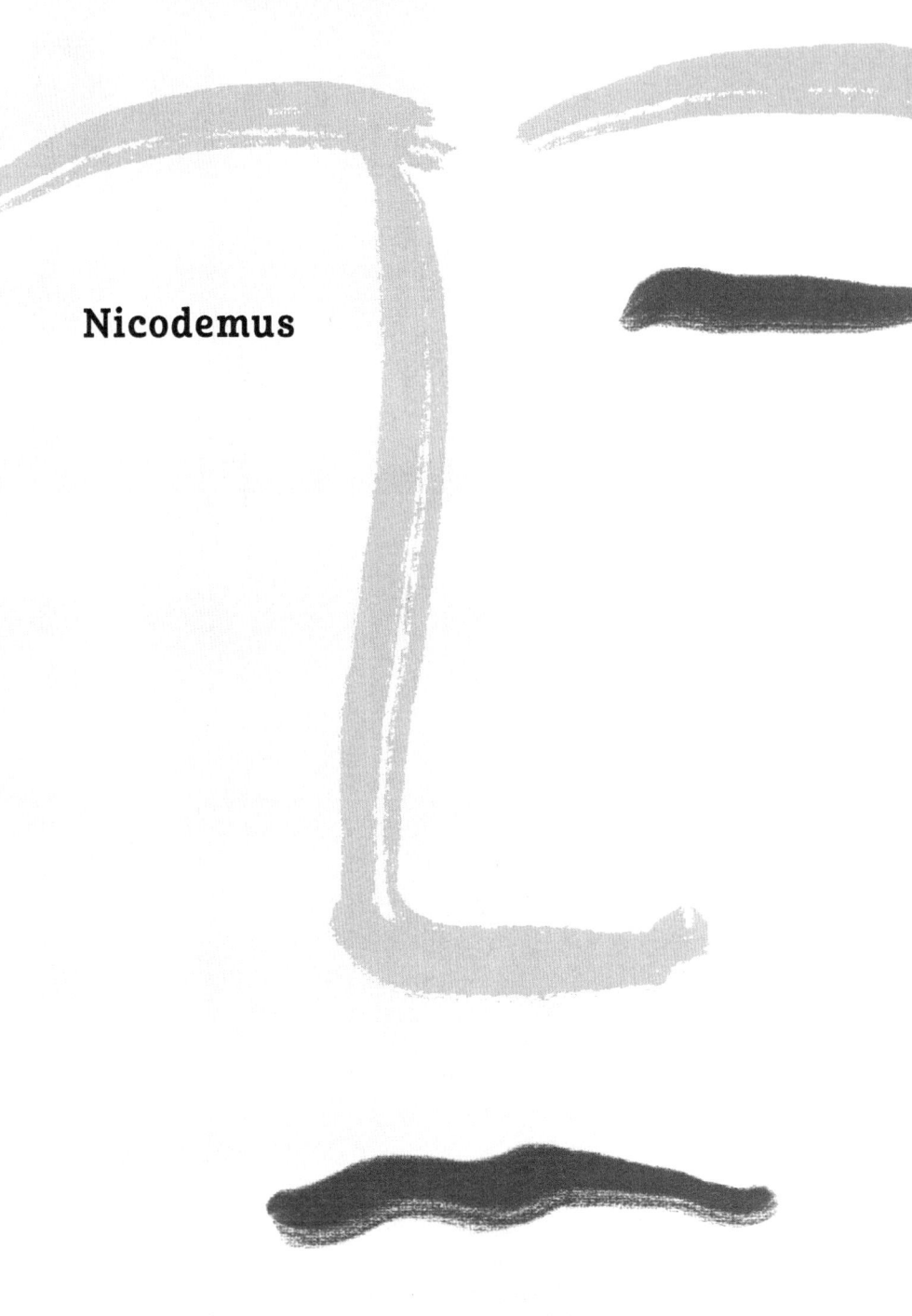

Nicodemus

Nicodemus

(John 3:1-21; 7:32-52; 19:38-42)

Nicodemus appears three times in the New Testament, all in John's Gospel. The best-known story shows Jesus telling him he needs to be "born from above" to see the kingdom of God. (Some translations of John 3:3 have "born again" and others have "born from above". Both ideas are contained in the original Greek.) Nicodemus is very interested in Christ. He says: "We know that you are a teacher who has come from God; for no one can do these signs that you do apart from the presence of God." We might be surprised to learn that he is a Pharisee, because in the Gospels Pharisees are often opposed to Jesus. Jesus calls them "hypocrites", "blind guides" and a "brood of vipers", among other things (Matthew 23:15, 16, 33). The Pharisees, for their part, are often shown asking Jesus trick questions with the intention of catching him out (12:10). They plot to get him arrested and plan on putting him to death (John 7:32; 11:45-53).

The Pharisees were a religious group known for their strict adherence to the Mosaic Law (the Ten Commandments and all the other regulations within the first five books of the Bible from Genesis to Deuteronomy). They have acquired a bad reputation as a result of their clashes with Christ. Look up the word "Pharisee" in most dictionaries and you will see that they are associated with hypocrisy and self-righteousness.

But do they deserve this reputation and how unusual was it for a Pharisee such as Nicodemus to be interested in Christ's teachings? Many modern scholars would argue that Pharisees have been represented unfairly and point out that they appear to have been popular and respected by ordinary people. Indeed, when Jesus called the Pharisees "hypocrites" he was unlikely to have meant they were not genuine in their beliefs or wholehearted in their attempts to keep the religious Law, for they took this very seriously. This is reflected in the life of Paul, the apostle who was a Pharisee before his conversion (Acts 26:5). He described them as "the strictest sect" of Judaism and talked of his "zeal" as a Pharisee, declaring himself to have been "blameless" in his "righteousness under the law" (Philippians 3:5-6). When Jesus called the Pharisees hypocrites, it was because they appeared to be good on the outside, but their law-keeping had not changed them within.[15]

Certainly, what we read about Nicodemus supports the notion that not all Pharisees opposed Christ, and other passages in the New Testament reflect this too. For instance, Luke records that Jesus was entertained in Pharisees' homes and shared meals with them on several occasions (7:36; 11:37; 14:1). Luke even tells us that it was Pharisees who warned Jesus about a plot King Herod was hatching to kill him (13:31). Pharisees also shared Jesus' belief in life after death, unlike their opponents the Sadducees. This may have meant that Jesus' message appealed more to Pharisees. Paul certainly tried to reach out to them by sharing his belief in Christ's resurrection (Acts 23:6-10).

While these references show that not all Jesus' interactions with Pharisees are negative, we cannot ignore the many Gospel passages which describe their opposition to him. Even Nicodemus is not presented as a wholehearted supporter. He comes to question Jesus at night, which could be a sign

that he doesn't want to make his interest in him public,
or could symbolise the spiritual darkness he is still in.
This suggests that although he is impressed with Jesus'
teaching and miraculous deeds, he is not yet a true believer.

So why is Nicodemus not fully convinced about Jesus?
John 9:16 might offer us a hint. It describes a dispute about
Jesus between some Pharisees. While some are impressed
with Jesus because of the miracles he's performed, others say,
"This man is not from God, for he does not observe the sabbath."
This suggests that it is Jesus' attitude to keeping laws, such as
what should or should not be done on the sabbath, that lies
at the heart of his differences with the Pharisees. This may also
be what made Nicodemus tentative about following him.

This dispute is in keeping with what we know about the
Pharisees, for conforming to the Mosaic Law was
fundamental to their beliefs. While Christians often criticise
Pharisees for being legalistic, there were good motives behind
their dedication to the Law. The Jews had suffered greatly
from conquest and oppression over the years. Probably the
most infamous example of this was the exile of 587 BC. The
Babylonian army had destroyed Jerusalem, razed the Temple
to the ground and forced many Jews to leave their homeland
to live in captivity in Babylon. Prophets such as Jeremiah and
Ezekiel declared this to be God's punishment for the people's
disobedience (Jeremiah 11:9-13; Ezekiel 14:21-23). The Pharisees
wanted to learn the lessons of the past to ensure that God
would not punish them again. Hence their desire to make
Israel a holy nation by encouraging the keeping of God's laws.
In addition, the political situation in the time of Jesus made
the Pharisees particularly concerned about Israel being led
astray again. Since 63 BC Israel had been ruled by the Romans.
The Pharisees knew that many other nations conquered by the

Romans had simply been swallowed up by the culture of their victors. Adherence to the letter of the Law was a way of ensuring that the Jews would stay faithful to the Lord in the face of the pagan culture in which they were immersed and so retain their identity as God's people.

The Pharisees believed that the Mosaic Law should be applied to every situation in life, but, as it often offered general principles rather than explicit instructions, they compiled an oral body of law to spell out exactly how to put these principles into practice. This is what the New Testament refers to as the "tradition of the elders" (Mark 7:3). To become a Pharisee, these men, who were often ordinary folk from all walks of life, would have to undergo a period of probation before making a pledge in front of a scribe to follow all the hundreds of rules and regulations that made up the oral law.[16]

To picture what this would mean in practice, let's take the fourth commandment, which forbids work on the sabbath. Keeping this important part of the Mosaic Law meant being clear and explicit as to exactly what counted as work. This involved working out how far one could travel: no more than a thousand yards (914 metres) from a person's home was considered acceptable, but any further counted as work.[17] Similarly, people needed to know how to care for their livestock on the sabbath. The oral law permitted them to give water to their animals on the sabbath, so long as it was in a trough and they did not hold a bucket up for the animal to drink from.[18] Such detailed prescription may seem odd to most of us, but it was motivated by a real concern to comply with the Law.

Jesus clashed with the Pharisees because, by focusing on the detail of these regulations, they missed the bigger picture. Helping people came second to following the rules, and that went against the true spirit of the Mosaic Law. So Jesus was prepared to break the Pharisees' rules, which said that healing on the sabbath was only acceptable when someone's life was in danger. He healed a man with a withered hand, a woman with a spinal deformity and a man with dropsy all on that day (Mark 3:1-6; Luke 13:10-17; 14:1-5). He was prepared to provoke and alienate many Pharisees because he disagreed with any interpretation of the Mosaic Law which involved leaving people to suffer any longer than necessary (Mark 3:1-5). He also criticised the Pharisees for being prepared to help animals on the sabbath but not people (Luke 13:15-16; 14:3-6).

It was not just over the sabbath rules that Jesus clashed with the Pharisees. The Gospels record him criticising their over-zealous tithing, saying that they meticulously tithed even tiny amounts of herbs, but neglected the more important principles of the Law: justice, mercy and faith (Matthew 23:23-24). Also, he did not follow Pharisaic codes around meals: he does not appear to have encouraged his disciples to ritually wash their hands before meals or to fast (Mark 7:1-5; Matthew 9:14). In particular he upset the Pharisees by sharing meals with people they considered sinners (Mark 2:15-17). This was something a Pharisee would never do, because for them eating a meal was a sign of fellowship and they did not want to be seen to be in communion with someone whose life was clearly not in line with God's will. Again, Jesus' main concern was for people. He ate with sinners to show them God's love in the hope of bringing them back to the Lord. It was a clash with the Pharisees over this very subject which caused Jesus to tell the parable of the prodigal son. In this story the elder son, who is angry with his father for forgiving and welcoming home his wayward brother, is commonly believed to represent the Pharisees.

In the parable of the tax collector and the Pharisee (Luke 18:9-14), Jesus highlights another pitfall of observing so many rules and regulations – the tendency for it to lead to pride. In his story the Pharisee boasts about fasting twice a week and tithing a tenth of all his income and thanks God that he is better than sinful people. However, rather than bringing him closer to God, his law-keeping had made him puffed up and arrogant and less aware of his unworthiness before the Lord. In contrast, Jesus described the humility of the tax collector, who did not even dare lift his eyes to heaven in prayer.

Perhaps it is just such over-confidence that explains Nicodemus' astonished response when Jesus tells him he needs to be "born from above" to experience the kingdom of God. At that time all but the most wicked Jews would expect to have a place in God's coming kingdom.[19] Therefore an upright man like Nicodemus, who was not only a law-abiding Pharisee but a leader and religious teacher, would certainly expect to be part of God's kingdom. No wonder he is shocked at the suggestion that even someone like him will have to start all over again (that is, be born again). But for Jesus entering the kingdom requires a transformation that only God's Spirit can achieve. Law-keeping alone is not able to bring the depth of righteousness that God desires, for it cannot change a person's inner nature; only a fresh start (being born again) with the power of God's Spirit (being born from above) can do that.

So what happened to Nicodemus after his meeting with Christ? We do not know what impact this conversation had on him, although his later appearances in John's Gospel suggest that he continued, at least, to be sympathetic towards Christ's cause. The next time we come across him is in John 7:32-52, where he is in the company of other Pharisees and chief priests. Jesus has been creating more controversy by his teaching in the Temple and the religious leaders have sent the Temple police to arrest him. The police are so enamoured by his teaching, however, that they return empty-handed, infuriating the Pharisees. Nicodemus then tries to calm the situation by encouraging his fellow Pharisees to give Jesus a fair hearing before rushing to bring him to judgement. His fellow leaders mock him and quip that he, like Jesus, must come from Galilee, for they can think of no other reason why he would stand up for Christ. Their flippancy suggests that they do not really believe Nicodemus to be a follower of Jesus, so if he has made any kind of commitment to him it is likely to have been secret.

John 3:1 refers to Nicodemus as "a leader of the Jews", suggesting that he was a member of the Jews' ruling council, their supreme court, the Sanhedrin. This is reinforced by the passage in chapter 7 when it says that Nicodemus "was one of them", meaning the group of chief priests and Pharisees who sent the Temple police to arrest Jesus. Men able to wield such power are likely to have been members of the Sanhedrin.[20]

Pharisees who were members of the Sanhedrin were also scribes, people who had undergone years of training and were responsible for interpreting the Mosaic Law and compiling their oral laws.[21] To have been a scribe, then, means that Nicodemus must have been a very learned man, which explains why Jesus refers to him as "a teacher of Israel" in John 3:10.

The Gospels describe scribes as wearing long robes embellished with tassels, so they would have been highly recognisable (Matthew 23:5; Luke 20:46). They wore distinctive white linen robes in contrast to the coloured clothes of ordinary folk and people stood up out of respect when they passed them in the street.[22] This is reflected in Jesus' words about scribes being honoured with the title "rabbi" when they were greeted in

the marketplace (Matthew 23:7). They were also used to being
given the best seats in the synagogues and at banquets (23:6).
We can, therefore, imagine Nicodemus as a distinguished
figure who was used to being treated with great honour.

The last mention of Nicodemus in John's Gospel is in 19:38-42.
Here he is associated with Joseph of Arimathea who was also
a member of the Sanhedrin (Luke 23:50-51). Interestingly,
Joseph is referred to as "a disciple of Jesus, though a secret
one because of his fear of the Jews". This makes one wonder
whether Nicodemus was also a secret disciple. As members
of the Sanhedrin, these men may have been involved in Jesus'
trial before the high priest, which ended in the decision to
send him on to the Roman procurator Pontius Pilate to be
condemned to death (Matthew 27:1-2). Luke's version (23:51)
makes it clear that although Joseph was part of the Sanhedrin
he did not approve of Jesus' death. If the words in Mark 14:64
are taken literally, that "all of [the Sanhedrin] condemned him
as deserving death", this means that they voted unanimously
against Jesus. If this is so, it suggests that Joseph of Arimathea
was absent from the vote. Was Nicodemus absent too? If not,
we are left with the unpalatable possibility that he voted
against Jesus.[23]

Is it conceivable that someone with sympathy for Jesus like
Nicodemus would have voted for Christ to be condemned?
Pressure from his fellow Pharisees, the angry frenzy of the trial,
the high priest's proclamation that Jesus was a blasphemer,
all make this possible, especially if Nicodemus still harboured
doubts about Jesus' attitude to the Law. Even if he absented
himself from the vote, Nicodemus is unlikely to have avoided
a troubled conscience. He must have wondered how differently
things could have turned out if he'd been there and spoken
up for Christ. Of course, Mark 14:64 might not be intended

literally and so the vote to condemn Jesus may not have been unanimous. In that scenario, Nicodemus could have voted to save Jesus, leaving us to wonder whether he spoke up for him, or remained silent.

All these possibilities become particularly intriguing when we consider what might have motivated Nicodemus to team up with Joseph of Arimathea after the crucifixion. It seems clear that by this point Joseph, at least, had come out of the shadows and was publicly identifying with Jesus, boldly asking the Roman procurator Pilate for permission to take his body down from the cross in order to place it in his tomb (John 19:38). It would be difficult to hide his discipleship after such an act. However, it is less certain whether Nicodemus' actions also reveal him to be a fully-fledged disciple. We are not told whether he went to Pilate with Joseph or helped him to move Jesus' body. However, we are told that he showed tremendous generosity in bringing an immense amount of expensive spices to anoint the body. He must have been an extremely wealthy man, for the weight of these spices would have been around thirty-three kilogrammes, more than five stone, an amount fit for anointing a king.[24] We are left wondering whether this generous act was a sign that Jesus' death had finally convinced Nicodemus to become a disciple, or whether it was simply the result of a guilty conscience at not having done more to prevent Christ's death.

Unfortunately, we do not know whether Nicodemus ever moved from an interest in Christ to full discipleship. Some scholars think he never became a Christian and believe that the main reason for including Nicodemus in the Gospel was as a warning message for Jews who were interested in Christ but did not have the courage to leave the synagogues and join the Church. Seen in this way, Nicodemus serves as a cautionary reminder that true faith should never be hidden.[25]

There is a tradition, though, that does offer a more hopeful view about Nicodemus' discipleship. He was held to have become a Christian and to have been driven from Jerusalem and given shelter by a man called Gamaliel, who is shown in Acts encouraging the Sanhedrin not to kill the apostles. The legend goes that in AD 415 Gamaliel appeared in a dream to a priest living twenty miles outside Jerusalem, revealing not only where his own tomb was, but also that of Nicodemus and the first Christian martyr, Stephen, who were buried nearby.[26] There is, however, little evidence for these traditions, although the scholar Richard Bauckham has carried out detailed research which suggests Nicodemus did become a disciple in the end. He believes that Nicodemus was part of an aristocratic Jerusalem family and was uncle to Naqdimon ben Gurion, an extremely wealthy and prominent member of the ruling class in the years before the Romans destroyed the city in AD 70. Most interestingly, he describes a list found in Jewish rabbinic material which names five disciples of Christ and believes that a couple of names on the list refer to Nicodemus. If Bauckham is correct, it would appear that Nicodemus really did find faith in the end.[27]

Perhaps, though, it is appropriate that we do not know for certain whether Nicodemus ever became a Christian, for he reflects the struggle that many like him would have had between the old ways of the Pharisees and the new ways that Jesus was bringing in. Jesus talked about the traditions of the Pharisees as old wine skins. In response to a question as to why his disciples did not fast like the Pharisees, he said, "no one puts new wine into old wineskins; otherwise, the wine will burst the skins" (Mark 2:22). Wine was kept in wine skins and older skins were not so flexible and so tended to burst when holding new wine, because it was still fermenting and producing gases. Jesus was bringing "new wine", a revolution which enabled people to go beyond the external forms of righteousness produced by law-keeping and be transformed from within by the Spirit. This necessitated breaking with the old ways and some Pharisees, such as Paul, eventually came around to accepting the new way. However, many of them, together with many other Jews, would not and as a result Judaism and Christianity would go their separate ways, Christianity becoming a religion in its own right. Which way Nicodemus went we do not know, but he would not have been alone in finding this a difficult choice.

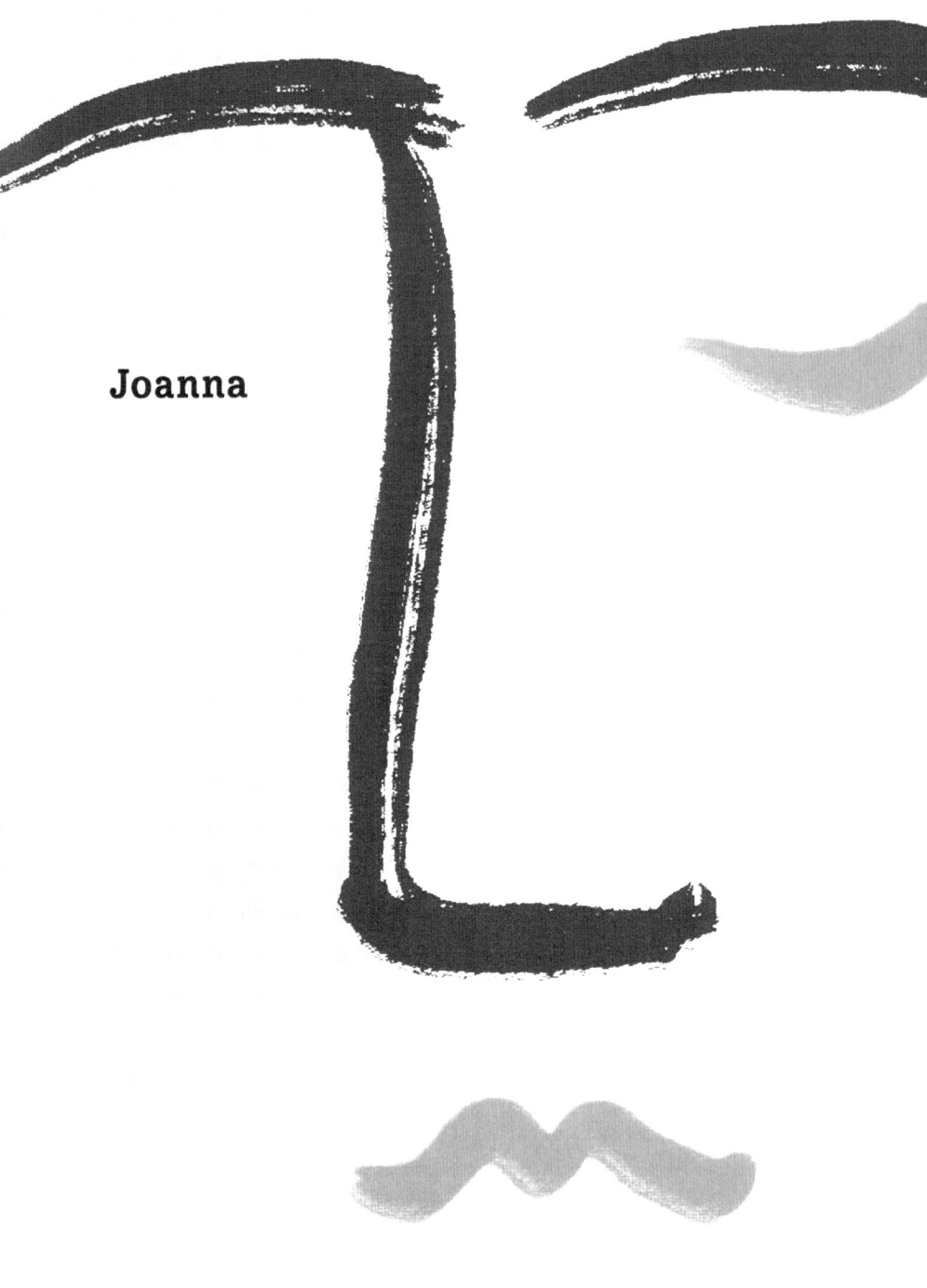

Joanna

Joanna

(Luke 8:1-3; 24:1-12)

When we imagine Jesus travelling around teaching and preaching, we probably envisage him accompanied by his twelve apostles. But a closer reading of Luke's Gospel, in particular, reveals a surprise. It was not just the Twelve who went around with Jesus, but a much larger group of people, who were also considered disciples. Luke 6:17, for instance, describes Jesus as standing "on a level place, with a great crowd of his disciples". Also, as he entered Jerusalem on a donkey, we are told "the whole multitude of the disciples began to praise God joyfully" (Luke 19:37. See also Luke 10:1 and John 6:60-67).

What might be even more surprising is that many of these disciples were women. Joanna was one of these female disciples who travelled around with Jesus, the Twelve and all his followers. We first learn about her in Luke 8:1-3. This is a fascinating little passage that offers us an intriguing insight into the makeup of the wider group of disciples. It begins by telling us that Jesus, "went on through cities and villages, proclaiming and bringing the good news of the kingdom". We then read:

> *The twelve were with him, as well as some women who had been cured of evil spirits and infirmities: Mary, called Magdalene, from whom seven demons had gone out, and Joanna, the wife of Herod's steward Chuza, and Susanna, and many others, who provided for them out of their resources.*

What the NRSV translation and most other versions do not make clear is that the Greek phrase translated as "many others" is in the feminine form, and so carries the meaning "many other women", which is how the Good News version translates it. Therefore, not only were Mary Magdalene, Joanna and Susanna disciples of Jesus, but many other women as well.

Luke introduces these female disciples much earlier on than the other Gospels. Mark and Matthew do not mention Jesus' women followers until his crucifixion when their sudden appearance comes out of the blue (Mark 15:40-41; Matthew 27:55-56). Luke, however, makes it clear that these women were with Jesus right from the start of his ministry, giving the impression that they remained with him throughout.

Luke 8:1*b*-3 is a difficult passage, because in the original Greek it is one long sentence, making it difficult to be sure who exactly did the providing out of their resources. Most scholars take these verses to mean that both the named and the unnamed women in the passage in some way "provided" for Jesus and probably the other disciples too. But it could be that Mary Magdalene, Joanna and Susanna were provided for by the unnamed women just as Jesus and the Twelve were.[28] This could suggest that these three women had particularly significant roles. In whatever way one reads this long sentence, though, it should not be taken to mean that the Twelve went around preaching with Jesus in contrast to the women who did the providing, as is often assumed, for Luke 8:1*a* shows that it was Christ alone doing the preaching, not Jesus and the Twelve. The main point of the passage seems to be not that the women were providing financially for the group but that, just like the men, they were disciples travelling around and spending time with Jesus.[29]

While the women's providing role was only one aspect of their discipleship, there is debate over exactly what they provided. Undoubtedly Jesus and his disciples would have needed financial support. Jesus appears to have had no income and the disciples had all left their livelihoods to follow him. Someone would have needed to pay for food and accommodation for the large group of people that were following Jesus by this point. Many, though, have doubted that women would have been able to provide such financial support. It is often assumed that they had little access to money of their own at this time and that the women provided for Jesus and the rest of the group in other ways, such as cooking, sewing and other domestic chores. However, some women did have access to money in a variety of ways: those without brothers could inherit wealth; well-off parents often made gifts to their daughters to ensure they were provided for when they died; widows and divorcees could be left money by their husbands, while some earned money using traditional skills, such as making clothes or bread.[30] In addition, the idea of the female disciples carrying out domestic chores does not sit well with the fact that they were not based in the home, but travelling around with Jesus from place to place.[31]

That women like Joanna travelled around with Jesus and a group of other men raises a lot of questions. It is often suggested that they must have been widows or single, because it is thought unlikely that husbands would be happy for their wives to leave the family and go off travelling with a group of men they were not related to. However, it would hardly have been considered appropriate for unmarried women to be travelling with Jesus. Indeed, some think it would have been scandalous for any woman to do so.[32]

While there is no mention of Mary of Magdalene or Susanna having husbands, Luke 8:3 states that Joanna was wife to a man named Chuza. This could simply mean that she was his widow and, if that were the case, Luke may have mentioned Chuza only as a way of explaining how Joanna was wealthy enough to provide for Jesus.[33] However, if she were still married to Chuza, then it is possible he may have been a believer, too, who was supportive of his wife doing this.

Chuza's job reveals more surprising information about the circumstances of the women who followed Christ. Luke tells us that Chuza was King Herod Antipas' steward (see page 70). This could mean that he was one of the many managers who looked after the king's various estates. However, Richard Bauckham argues that, as Joanna knew Jesus from the start of his ministry in Galilee, it is probable that the couple were based there and, since Herod had no estates in Galilee, this might mean that Chuza was not an estate manager but had an even grander role, as "finance minister of the kingdom". If so, he would probably have been based at the King's palace in Tiberias, a city built on the shore of the Sea of Galilee, where he would have held very high office and been part of the royal court. Bauckham also says that Chuza was a Nabatean name, suggesting he originated from Arabia. Interestingly, King Herod's first wife was a Nabatean princess. (It was this princess that Herod Antipas later divorced to marry his sister-in-law; an act which provoked John the Baptist's fiery criticism and ultimately led to his execution.) Therefore, it is possible that Chuza first arrived in Galilee as part of the princess's entourage.[34]

Joanna must have been a radical and dedicated follower of Christ, then. Not only was she a woman travelling with Jesus and other men, which would have been highly unusual, if not completely scandalous, but she was also a wealthy woman of high status. Yet it appears that she was prepared to leave all her wealth and status behind to go on the road with people whom most others of her class would consider riff-raff: poor, common folk, many of whom had dubious reputations. This shows how the Gospel brought together people from a wide range of very different backgrounds.

The inclusive nature of this new community is not only reflected in Joanna's attitude towards her fellow disciples, but in their acceptance of her. Members of the court of Herod Antipas would not have been popular with most ordinary Jews. He did not have a good reputation and was seen as a traitor for collaborating with the Romans. As well as this, he had built the city of Tiberias, where his court was based, over a cemetery, although some believed that this went against their religious laws. To make matters worse, his subjects would have been forced to pay high taxes to pay for the city to be built. When it was built, its opulence, cosmopolitan Roman ways and laxity of religious observance created an uncomfortable contrast to the villages around. So Joanna's association with Herod could have made her very unpopular among her fellow Jews.[36]

So what caused Joanna to step out of the comfort of her wealthy, high-status life to join a group of people who differed from her in so many ways? Luke 8:2 tells us that Jesus had healed Joanna at some point earlier in his ministry. Maybe she had sought out Christ because she was desperate for healing, and either the miracle she experienced, or the impact of meeting Jesus face to face, was enough to inspire her to leave everything behind and follow him.

Joanna's commitment to Jesus was so strong it appears to have given her the courage to stay faithful to him, even when many others fled and abandoned him after his arrest. She is next mentioned by name in Luke's account of the empty tomb (24:10). It also seems reasonable to assume that she was one of the women Luke describes "who had followed him from Galilee" and "stood at a distance, watching" the crucifixion, and also that she was among "the women who had come with him from Galilee", who followed Joseph of Arimathea and watched him lay Jesus' body in the tomb (Luke 23:49, 55).

L uke 24:1-12 mentions Joanna as one of the women who witnessed the empty tomb. Her dedication to Christ led her, together with Mary Magdalene and Mary the mother of James, to go to the tomb with the intention of anointing Jesus' body with spices – something there was not time for them to do before the sabbath. When they arrived they were shocked to find the entrance stone rolled away and the body gone. Two angelic visitors appeared and told them to: "Remember how he told you, while he was still in Galilee, that the Son of Man must be handed over to sinners, and be crucified, and on the third day rise again" (verses 6-7). This shows that Jesus had clearly taught the women, not just the twelve apostles, important information about his death and resurrection. The women, then, were at the centre of what was going on and were vital witnesses not only of Jesus' death and resurrection, but his teaching and life too.

Indeed, the women's role as witnesses is vitally important to Luke. As we have seen, he makes it clear that Joanna and the other women "who had followed him from Galilee" were disciples of Jesus from the start of his ministry and continued to be with him throughout. They were, then, witnesses of his teaching and miracles in Galilee, and followed him on the seventy-mile trip to Jerusalem, where they witnessed his death, saw Joseph of Arimathea place him in his tomb and later found the same tomb empty. Joanna was also one of the women who acted as a witness to the apostles, telling them about the resurrection. She told them that Jesus had risen again, although Luke also tells us Peter and the other male disciples did not believe her, thinking it "an idle tale" (24:11). William Barclay says the meaning of the Greek is much blunter than this and that Luke uses a contemporary medical word to describe "the babbling of a fevered and insane mind".[37] It seems likely, then, that the apostles' disbelief was at least partly due to the news having been reported to them by women. Women's testimonies were less likely to be believed because they were often considered too emotional and irrational.[38] Indeed, the second-century Greek philosopher Celsus rejected the claims of Christianity on the basis that the resurrection was witnessed by "a half-frantic woman".[39]

In contrast to Celsus, many people now would argue that the very fact the Gospels record women as the first witnesses of the resurrection confirms the authenticity of this event. If the resurrection was a made-up tale, why would those who came up with the story choose women to be its first witnesses, when they were far less likely than men to be believed? It is also encouraging for women that, despite the prevalence of such prejudice, God still chose to entrust the news of the resurrection to them first.

It also seems likely that Joanna's role as a witness had an impact on the material we have in the New Testament. There is information about Herod that is only found in Luke's Gospel and many scholars think that she may well have been the source because of her close links with Herod's court. Did Joanna, for instance, give Luke reports about Herod Antipas' interest in Jesus and his trial before Herod? (9:9*b*; 23:4-12). Was she one of the eyewitnesses Luke relied upon when putting his Gospel together? (1:2).

Similarly, Luke is the only Gospel to mention Joanna at the empty tomb, whereas Mary the mother of James and Mary Magdalene are mentioned by other Gospel writers. Does this mean that Joanna was the source of Luke's empty tomb account? If so, we may owe Joanna a huge debt.

Joanna's role as witness to Christ may have gone beyond even this. There are good reasons for believing that she is mentioned again later in the Bible and that she could be the same person as Junia who is greeted by Paul at the end of his letter to the church in Rome (Luke 16:7): "Greet Andronicus and Junia, my relatives who were in prison with me; they are prominent among the apostles, and they were in Christ before I was."

To claim that Joanna was the same person as Junia may, at first, seem strange. How can Joanna be Junia when they have completely different names? Richard Bauckham points out, however, that Jews did sometimes take a second name that was Greek or less commonly Roman, often one that sounded like their Semitic name. He says early Christian missionaries (who were Jewish) may have chosen Roman or Greek names when working among Gentiles as they felt this to be more "culturally appropriate"; easier for the people they were trying to reach to understand. Joanna, with her connection to Herod's court, may well have had a Roman name, possibly choosing Junia because it was similar in sound to Joanna.[40]

Those who have older Bible translations may be even more puzzled by this suggestion, for some will not have the female name Junia, but the male name Junias. There is a fascinating history behind this. Greek nouns have endings that are either masculine, feminine or neutral. The name that has been translated as Junia/Junias has an ending in Romans 16:7 that could be either masculine or feminine. It seems that until the thirteenth century the female name Junia was the usual translation, with good reason.[41] There are a few hundred examples of the female name in Latin and Greek inscriptions, but none of the male name.[42] In addition, the vast majority of the early Church Fathers (theologians of the Church in the first seven or so centuries of Christianity) considered the name female. It seems that the male name came to be used instead of the female simply because Romans 16:7 describes Andronicus and Junia as being "prominent among the apostles", and medieval commentators assumed that a prominent apostle could not have been a woman.

In addition, there are those who accept the name is female, but cannot accept that a woman would have been an apostle. They tend to favour translations of the verse that describe Junia in terms of being "well known *to* the apostles" rather than "well known *among* the apostles".[43] However, this is not the view of many modern commentators who think this is not the best way to understand the Greek.[44] Certainly the early Church Fathers did not take it that way. The fourth-century Church Father, Chrysostom, for instance, seemed to have had no problem believing there had been a female apostle called Junia, for he wrote, "Indeed, how great the wisdom of this woman must have been that she was even deemed worthy of the title of apostle".[45]

So what evidence is there for Joanna being Junia the apostle and what did Paul mean by calling her an apostle in the first place? Bauckham points out that Paul describes Junia (and Andronicus, with whom she is associated) as his "relatives", by which he believes Paul probably meant that they were fellow Jews rather than blood relatives. He also argues that Paul's assertion that "they were in Christ before I was", shows that they were Palestinian Jews and members of the early Church in Jerusalem.[46] All this fits with Joanna.

But what did Paul mean by "apostle"? It is often assumed that this is a term which describes only the twelve apostles. However, Paul had a broader definition. He considered someone an apostle if they had seen the risen Lord and had been commissioned by Christ. This is why Paul could call himself an apostle despite not being one of the Twelve, for he had seen the risen Lord at his conversion on the Damascus Road and was commissioned by him (Acts 9:1-5; 22:6-11; 26:12-18). Paul would not have called someone an apostle lightly, for his letters show that he often had to defend his right to be called apostle against critics who felt he should not refer to himself that way (1 Corinthians 9:1-2; Galatians 1:11 – 2:10).

So if a fundamental attribute of an apostle was to have seen the risen Lord, this is a criterion that Joanna could have met. Not only was she at the empty tomb, but it seems reasonable to assume that she remained with the other disciples in Jerusalem and was one of the "companions" mentioned in Luke 24:33, the apostles who witnessed the resurrection appearance, as well as the commissioning and promise of the Spirit at the ascension (verses 44-53), as these all follow on from one another. In addition, not only did they become Christians before Paul, but as Romans 16:7 says, they were in prison with Paul and therefore had suffered as he had for his apostleship.

If Joanna was, indeed, the same person as Junia, she appears to have been responsible for building up the church in Rome. She may have been sent to Rome as a missionary and laboured in the city for a decade, building up the church there while Paul focused on growing churches further east in Greece and Asia Minor, which could be another reason why Paul referred to her as "prominent among the apostles".[48] As Professor James Dunn puts it:

Andronicus and Junia are the only apostles Paul mentions in regard to the Roman Christians. So the most likely explanation is that Andronicus and Junia were the apostles who founded (one or more of) the house church(es) in Rome.[49]

But who was Andronicus, linked to Junia in Romans 16:7? Most commentators think he was her husband. But as we have seen, Luke 8:3 says that Joanna was married to Chuza. So does this rule out the theory that Joanna was Junia? Not necessarily, for it is, of course, possible that Joanna was Chuza's widow and he had died before she started travelling with Jesus, or that he died later. Andronicus, then, would have been her second husband. Or he may not have been her husband, but her brother or another relative.

Unfortunately, we do not know how Joanna's life ended. If she was indeed Junia, there is a possibility that she remained in Rome and was caught up in Nero's bloody persecution of the Christians there. Orthodox tradition holds that she went to Hungary with Andronicus, who it is claimed became Bishop of Pannonia. Here, tradition has it, they healed diseases, cast out demons and were martyred.[50]

We do know that Joanna was a brave and impressive disciple of Christ who witnessed his life, death and resurrection, and may well have passed on what she saw and heard, not only to people in her own lifetime but to us today, by being one of Luke's sources for his Gospel. She faithfully supported Christ financially so he could carry out his ministry and stuck by him even when others, fearing for their own lives after his arrest, fled. She was prepared to give up her privileged lifestyle and go against social convention to travel with Jesus and the poor, low-status individuals who followed him, probably facing severe criticism for doing so.

And if Joanna was the same person as Junia, her dedication may have taken her all the way to Rome where she worked as an apostle telling others what she had seen. If she was responsible for starting up the Roman Church, then she did a tremendous job. It is estimated that the number of Christians in that city was around 1,400 only a couple of decades after Jesus' death and her work continued to bear fruit beyond her lifetime, for it is thought that two hundred years later there were more than a million Christians in Rome.[51] If Joanna was indeed the apostle Junia, then she really did play a very significant part in church history.

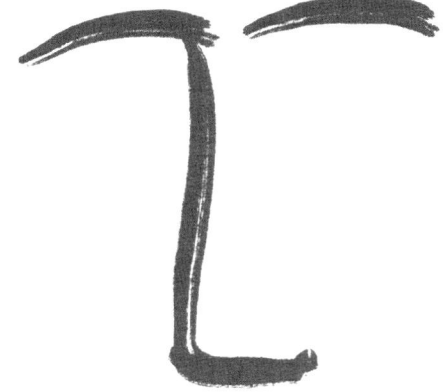

Herod the Great
and his
descendants

Herod the Great
and his descendants

The Bible uses the name Herod when talking of several different men: Herod the Great, his son Herod Antipas and his grandson Herod Agrippa I. As well as all these, Herod the Great's other sons Herod Philip and Herod Archelaus also get a mention, as does his great grandson Herod Agrippa II, although they are not referred to as Herod in the Bible. There are some fascinating characters among these rulers and learning about them helps us better understand the world of Jesus and his first followers. We are fortunate to have the writings of the first-century Jewish historian Josephus, which tell us a great deal about Herod and his descendants and much of the information in this chapter comes from his works.

Herod the Great, 40 - 4 BC[52]
(referred to in the Bible as Herod)
(Matthew 2)

Herod the Great reigned over an area that included Galilee, Judaea, Samaria and Idumaea.

This Herod is best known for ordering the slaughter of all boys aged two and under in Bethlehem and its surroundings. Matthew 2 describes Magi, wise men from the east, arriving in Israel. They had been following a star which they believed to be a sign: a child had been born who was destined to be king of the Jews. As Herod was the Jewish king at that time, it made him understandably jumpy. Many people wanted him dethroned, so any talk of a competing king was a direct threat. He asked the wise men to let him know where the baby was as soon as they had found him, pretending he too wanted to pay homage to the child. It was when the Magi slipped away without revealing the child's whereabouts that a furious Herod ordered this horrific massacre. Scripture predicted that the Messiah, the great ruler the Jews longed for, would come from Bethlehem, so he sent his soldiers there to slaughter the "innocents", as they are known, in the hope that Jesus would be among them. Such cruelty was not uncharacteristic of this king, as we shall learn later. He was deeply insecure about his throne and this had already driven him to do many awful things to hold on to it.

Herod's insecurity stemmed from his deep unpopularity. Despite being king of the Jews, he was not an independent monarch but ruled on behalf of the Romans. He is what is called a client king: someone loyal to Rome who had been appointed to ensure that the people remained subservient to the empire. Many Jews resented him for serving their oppressors.

Herod would never have been king if it were not for the Romans. They had seized direct control over the country in 63 BC, effectively ending a period of independence for Jews under their own rulers, the Hasmoneans. The Hasmoneans were much loved by the Jews, for this royal family was established by the Maccabees, a group of freedom fighters who had fought hard and had won a rare time of liberty for their nation.

In 40 BC, twenty-three years after the Roman conquest, the Hasmoneans managed to briefly regain independence from Rome. When the Parthians, from ancient Iran, drove the Romans out of Judaea they made their ally Antigonus, the Jewish son of a previous Hasmonean ruler, king of Judaea.[53] At the time,

Herod was tetrarch (governor) of Judaea and, being a politician
serving the Romans, he was forced to flee. He made his way to
Rome where the Senate gave him the task of regaining control
over Judaea, declaring him to be King of the Jews. However,
he had to fight for his new kingdom. Over the next three years,
he regained Galilee, Samaria and Idumaea and conquered Judaea,
laying siege to Jerusalem for a number of months. At the end of
a bloody campaign that cost the lives of many of his own people,
Herod had gained his kingdom and Antigonus, last of the Jewish
Hasmonean rulers, had been executed by the Romans. Herod,
then, began his rule with the blood of his own people on his
hands, which did nothing to endear him to his subjects.

Herod was also unpopular because many of his people did
not consider him a proper Jew. His family were from Idumaea,
an area south of Judaea, which had fairly recently been
conquered by the Jews. As a result, many Idumaeans had
converted to Judaism. These Idumaean Jews were commonly
viewed as only half-Jewish: "alien by blood but Jewish by
religion".[54] Not only was Herod one of these so-called "half-Jews",
but he came from a family with no pedigree or royal blood.
His father, Antipater, had worked his way up from nothing by
means of his great political skills, collaborating with the Romans
to gain significant power and influence for himself and his family.
It is not hard to imagine the resentment the Jews felt towards
Herod. He was not only a foreigner with no claim to the throne,
but someone who had deposed Antigonus who, as a descendant
of their Maccabee heroes, they considered the rightful king.

Herod was acutely aware of his unpopularity and sought
to win his people over. He was careful to follow Jewish
religious laws and insisted that any Gentile man marrying into
his family was circumcised.[55] To try and give himself more
legitimacy he married Mariamme, granddaughter of two
Hasmonean kings, John Hyrcanus II and Aristobulus II.

Herod was very much in love with Mariamme, but despite the marriage being intended to shore up his throne, it only added to his insecurity. His sons, Alexander and Aristobulus descended from the Hasmonean line through their mother, were more popular with the people than Herod. In addition, Mariamme brought other tensions into Herod's household. His relatives despised her because she looked down on them for their lack of royal breeding. On her part, Mariamme believed Herod was behind the death of her grandfather, John Hyrcanus II, as well as her brother, a belief that would do little to foster a happy marriage. In addition, Antipater, Herod's eldest son by another of his wives (named after his grandfather), plotted against his half-brothers, Alexander and Aristobulus, to ensure he would be Herod's heir.

In this poisonous court atmosphere false accusations of adultery were made against Mariamme by her enemies, driving the possessive Herod mad with jealousy. Even though he was still in love with her, he ordered her execution – a decision that seems to have sent him temporarily insane with grief and guilt. However, this guilt did not prevent him going on to treat her sons Alexander and Aristobulus in exactly the same way. He wrongly believed they were plotting to take his throne and, though they were not found guilty of a capital offence in court, Herod had them strangled. And that was not the end of his slaughter. Days before his own death, he ordered the execution of his scheming elder son Antipater, too. No wonder Emperor Augustus, alluding to Herod's strict religious avoidance of pork, reportedly said, "It is better to be Herod's pig than his son".[57]

Herod, then, was one paranoid man. In the light of this, as the Christian political theorist Alan Storkey puts it, for wise men to come to Jerusalem asking about a new king of the Jews "would be slightly less safe than putting your head into the mouth of a lion and asking what was for lunch."[58] However, because there is no record outside the Bible of Herod's slaughter of young children in Bethlehem, some scholars have questioned whether such an event ever happened. Yet such cruel behaviour seems totally in keeping with other terrible acts ordered by Herod. This was a man so cruel that, as he lay dying, he commanded all leading citizens to be shut in the hippodrome so that on his death they could be slaughtered with darts because he knew that would be the only way there would be any genuine tears shed at his passing. And, as we have already seen, he was so possessive of his throne that he killed three of his own sons and his wife along with many others to secure it. The behaviour Matthew records seems entirely in keeping with his character. As Josephus says, Herod was a man "of great barbarity towards all men equally, and a slave to his passions".[59]

It is also true that, despite his terrible flaws, Herod had many skills. Like his father before him he was a clever politician as well as an impressive soldier. He also brought the Jews a period of peace, stability and prosperity, albeit under Roman rule. Perhaps, though, his most impressive achievement was his stunning building work, much of which was carried out to try and win over the Jewish people. Among many projects he built the city of Caesarea on the Mediterranean coast with its impressive artificial harbour and aqueducts, the higher of which was over five miles long and supplied the city with water from springs on Mount Carmel.[60] It was in this city that Paul was put on trial before being sent to Rome (Acts 23:23-35). The palace fortress at Herodium, around seven miles from Jerusalem, was another significant achievement of Herod's, built high on a hill and approached by two hundred steps. In 2007 the archaeologist Ehud Netzer claimed to have discovered Herod's tomb at Herodium made from a beautifully decorated red-tinged limestone. Unfortunately this tomb was discovered in pieces and Jewish studies expert Geza Vermes has speculated that it may have been smashed up by Jewish rebels fuelled by their hatred for Herod.[61]

But Herod's greatest achievement of all was the one most intended to win Jewish hearts. He rebuilt the Temple in Jerusalem, making it far grander and more elaborate. This was a massive undertaking. Although he began the work in 19 BC, it was not finished until fifty-nine years after his death in AD 63, ironically only seven years before it would be razed to the ground by the Romans.

The Temple was Herod's greatest achievement. Josephus, who would have seen this magnificent building with his own eyes, described its beauty, saying it was made of white stone that made it look from a distance like a snow-capped mountain. He also wrote that it was adorned with gold and reflected the sun so strongly that people could hardly look at it.

Jesus' disciples were clearly impressed with the Temple, too, which was still being constructed in their time. One of them gazed admiringly at it and said to Jesus, "Look, Teacher, what large stones and what large buildings!" (Mark 13:1). Their astonishment is not surprising, for some of the stones used to build the platform the Temple stood upon were forty feet long, twelve feet high and eighteen feet wide.[62] It was an astounding feat of engineering.

Herod was also associated with some people very well known from history, most notably Mark Anthony and Cleopatra. He was very friendly with Anthony but was not enamoured with Cleopatra and felt she was not a trustworthy ally for his friend. It has been claimed that she tried unsuccessfully to seduce Herod and, insulted by his rejection, took a dislike to him.[63]

Herod is recorded as suffering a horrible end. Josephus has a particularly vivid description of the final days of his illness, which he believed was punishment for wrongdoing. He wrote that Herod's feet and abdomen swelled with fluid, his breath stank, his bowels ulcerated, and his genitals rotted and became infested with worms. Of course, the gruesome details may well have been exaggerated, to show that Herod got what he deserved.

After Herod died, his kingdom was divided between three of his sons: Herod Archelaus, Herod Philip and Herod Antipas (not to be confused with Herod's other son, Antipater, whom he executed). Unlike their father, none of Herod's sons was honoured with the title "king" but rather they were referred to as "ethnarch" in Archelaus' case, or "tetrarch" in the case of the other two. These were titles given to more minor rulers. All three sons are mentioned in the New Testament.

Herod Archelaus, 4 BC – AD 6
(referred to in the Bible as Archelaus)
(Matthew 2:19-23)

Archelaus was given Judaea, which included the capital Jerusalem, to rule. He is mentioned in relation to Mary and Joseph's decision not to return to Judaea. The couple had fled to Egypt when Herod the Great, his father, sought to kill the baby Jesus. However, Matthew says that after the death of Herod the Great, Joseph had a dream in which he was told to return to Israel. We also read, though, that when Joseph "heard that Archelaus was ruling over Judaea in place of his father Herod, he was afraid to go there. And after being warned in a dream, he went away to the district of Galilee", making the town of Nazareth his home. Galilee to the north of Judaea was ruled, as we shall see later, by another of Herod's sons, Antipas.

So, what was it about Archelaus that made Joseph so wary? Even before his reign had been officially approved by the Roman emperor, Augustus, there was trouble. Protests began in the capital, the cause of which stemmed back to Archelaus' father's controversial decision to put to death some men who had pulled down a statue of an eagle (the emblem of imperial Rome) from the gate of the Temple. Grievances turned to rioting and three thousand protestors were killed by Archelaus' troops in the Temple. Like his father before him, he began his rule with the blood of his own people on his hands.

Josephus records that Archelaus was so unpopular with his fellow Jews that, after ten years of his reign, Jewish leaders complained to Augustus about his bad treatment of his people. It appears that Archelaus had already been warned to be temperate in his behaviour, and as a result of his people's complaints he was removed from his position and exiled to Gaul. The Jews must have hated him a great deal to have preferred direct Roman rule to being governed by one of their own. From that point on, Judaea was ruled directly by Rome through prefects rather than a Jewish client king, which is why we find Pontius Pilate in control of Jerusalem at the time of Jesus' trial.

There is another reference in the Bible that could allude to Archelaus. In Luke 19:11-27 Jesus tells a parable about a nobleman who "went to a distant country to get royal power for himself and then return". This is exactly what Archelaus did on the death of his father: he travelled to Rome to ask to be made king in accordance with his father's will. The parable continues, "But the citizens of his country hated him and sent a delegation after him, saying, 'We do not want this man to rule over us.'" This had happened in Archelaus' case too. Josephus records that after Herod's death a group of Jews went to Rome unsuccessfully to beg Augustus not to install Archelaus as their new ruler. Jesus was clearly using an illustration from the political life of his nation to teach truths about the kingdom of God.

Herod Philip, 4 BC – AD 33/34
(referred to in the Bible as Philip)
(Luke 3:1)

Philip inherited the least desirable portion of his father's kingdom. His territory was an area north-east of Galilee, the best-known part of which was the city of Caesarea Philippi mentioned in the Bible as the place where Peter confessed Jesus to be the Messiah (Matthew 16:13-16). After having made improvements to the city, Philip changed its name from Paneas to Caesarea Philippi, adding his own name to it to distinguish it from the city of Caesarea his father had built on the coast.[64]

Philip seems to have been a good ruler. In contrast to Archelaus, Josephus refers to him as someone who was quiet and moderate, both in his personal life and as a ruler.[65]

In the Bible, we only read about Philip in Luke's Gospel (3:1) where we are told that it was during his rule that John the Baptist began baptising and preaching around the River Jordan. Philip has another connection to the Baptist, too: he was married to Salome, the daughter of Herodias who was Herod Antipas' wife. Salome is, of course, infamous for demanding the head of John the Baptist on a platter.

Herod Antipas, 4 BC – AD 39
(referred to in the Bible as Herod)
(Matthew 14:5; Mark 6:14-29; Luke 13:31)

Herod Antipas is mentioned in the Bible far more than any other of Herod the Great's descendants. This is because he was tetrarch of Galilee where Jesus carried out much of his ministry. He is most famous for his altercation with John the Baptist, who railed against him for marrying his brother's wife, Herodias. Herodias was the daughter of Aristobulus, Antipas' half-brother, who was murdered on the orders of their father, Herod the Great. The story of Antipas' dealings with the Baptist can be read in Mark 6:14-29.

Antipas had been married for at least two decades to the daughter of King Aretas IV of Nabatea. However, when Antipas was staying with his half-brother, Philip (a different Philip from the tetrarch discussed earlier), he took a fancy to his wife, Herodias. She agreed to leave her husband and marry Antipas, so long as he abandoned his current Nabatean wife, which he agreed to do. The Baptist was outraged by such behaviour and many would have shared his anger, for this Jewish ruler was, in their eyes, breaking God's laws in two ways: by divorcing his wife without good cause and by marrying his sister-in-law.[66] Indeed, Jesus may have had the royal couple in mind when he likened remarriage following divorce to adultery in Mark 10:11-12.[67]

Antipas had the Baptist thrown in prison in the hill fortress of Machaerus. William Barclay describes this place as "one of the loneliest and grimmest and most unassailable fortresses in the world".[68] However, despite his treatment of John, Antipas was fascinated by the preacher. The account in Mark's Gospel (6:19-20) suggests that it was Herodias who "had a grudge against" John and wanted him dead, whereas Antipas himself seems to have been in awe of John and "protected him" from her. Indeed, when Antipas heard the Baptist, "he was greatly perplexed; and yet he liked to listen to him".

It is unsurprising that Herodias would feel particularly threatened by John, for if Antipas had listened to him and separated from her, she would have lost everything. However, Herodias got her opportunity to strike when her daughter, Salome, pleased Antipas and his guests so much by dancing at a banquet, that he foolishly promised to give her whatever she wanted. After consulting with her mother she asked for the head of John the Baptist "on a platter", and reluctantly Antipas agreed.

Condemnation of this act appears to have been widespread: the Baptist was a respected figure. Josephus says that when King Aretas IV defeated Antipas in battle, a number of Jews took this to be God's judgement on him for killing a righteous man. Jesus, too, seems to have thought little of Antipas and, as the Baptist was a relative, this is not surprising. Luke 13:31-32 records him referring to Antipas as "that fox".

Jesus did, in fact, meet Antipas later. Antipas was on a pilgrimage to Jerusalem at the time of Christ's trial before the Roman procurator Pontius Pilate. When Pilate realised that Jesus was from Galilee, under Antipas' jurisdiction, he paid the tetrarch the courtesy of involving him in Christ's trial (Luke 23:6-12). This was significant, as up until that point the two men had been enemies, probably because Pilate had ordered the slaughter of some of Antipas' subjects, Galilean pilgrims who had travelled to Jerusalem (Luke 13:1).

Antipas appears to have had the same mixed feelings about Jesus as he had about John the Baptist. We are told that at the trial Antipas "was very glad" to see Jesus. He had clearly been aware of him for a while, for Luke tells us that Antipas "had been wanting to see him for a long time, because he had heard about him and was hoping to see him perform some sign" (23:8).

Mark's Gospel (6:16) reports that Antipas thought that Jesus was John risen from the dead. This suggests he was struggling with a guilty conscience over killing him. Yet despite this he also planned to kill Jesus (Luke 13:31). This may have been for the same reason his father sought to murder him as a baby: fear that he might one day lead an uprising and seize his crown. It was not necessarily an unfounded fear. After feeding the five thousand, Jesus had to withdraw because many people wanted to force him to be king (John 6:15). It is possible that some of those involved in this potential uprising may have been armed Jewish freedom fighters.[69]

Antipas was to be disappointed, though, by his much-anticipated meeting with Jesus, who refused to talk to him, let alone perform the miracles he had hoped to see (Luke 23:9). Again, his mixed feelings towards Jesus are reflected. He went against the chief priests and scribes in finding him not guilty and sent him back to Pilate (verses 14-15). This may have been because he did not want to overstep the mark and disagree with Pilate, who had ultimate jurisdiction in Jerusalem and had already said he could find no basis for the charges against Jesus. Despite finding Christ innocent, we are told Antipas and his soldiers "treated him with contempt and mocked him" and "put an elegant robe on him" before returning him to Pilate (verse 11).

The report of Antipas' meeting with Jesus is found only in Luke's Gospel. It is believed that Luke had contact with a number of people from Antipas' court who had become Christians, and this is how he had been able to obtain this information about the tetrarch. Luke 8:3, for instance, tells us about Joanna, a follower of Christ whose husband Chuza was steward to Antipas (see also chapter 4). Luke also tells us in the Acts of the Apostles (13:1) about Manaen from the church at Antioch who was a member of Antipas' court. It is thought that he was actually Antipas' foster brother and had been brought up with him as his companion.[70] It may have been through these people that Antipas first heard about Jesus and became intrigued by him.

Antipas' rule ended abruptly as a result of more scheming from his wife, Herodias. Her brother Agrippa I had been made king over Herod Philip's old territory and she did not see why her husband, a tetrarch, should not also have a royal title. Just as she had done years before about John the Baptist, she nagged her reluctant husband, pushing him into going to Rome to ask the emperor to make him a king as well. Unfortunately for Antipas, his brother-in-law Agrippa got wind of his plans and, as the two of them had fallen out, stirred up trouble for Antipas with the emperor. He informed Emperor Caligula that Antipas had stored up enough armour for seventy thousand men and was planning to rebel against Rome. Antipas was exiled to Gaul, where he is thought to have been assassinated.[71]

Because her brother, Agrippa, was an ally of Caligula's, Herodias was offered the option of escaping her husband's exile, but she chose to go with Antipas. Josephus has little sympathy for her, saying that her banishment was punishment from God for envying her brother. He also felt that Antipas' fate was God's judgement, for having listened to such a woman. Herodias' hounding of her husband led, then, not only to the death of John the Baptist, but also, ironically, to the humiliating demise of Antipas himself.

Herod Agrippa I, AD 41-44
(referred to in the Bible as Herod)
(Acts 12)

Agrippa I was Herod the Great's grandson and the child of Aristobulus (one of the sons whom Herod had slain). He was also, as we have already seen, brother to Antipas' wife Herodias. We read about him in Acts 12 where he is held responsible for the execution "with the sword" of Jesus' disciple James and the imprisonment of Peter. This same chapter tells, too, of Agrippa's own dramatic death.

Agrippa's life involved a sensational reversal of fortune. As a child he was sent to be educated in Rome, where he managed to accumulate large amounts of debt and make enemies. He seems to have spent a lot of time fleeing his debtors. He also fell out with his brother-in-law, Herod Antipas, even though Antipas had provided him with a job as a magistrate in Tiberias to help him out of his financial troubles. Consequently, he lost that job and was forced to move on again, eventually ending up back in Italy.

Things seemed to improve for Agrippa for a time. The Emperor Tiberius lent him money and he became friends with the emperor's great-nephew, Caligula.[72] However, a foolish conversation on a chariot ride with his friend led to disaster. He told Caligula that he hoped his friend would soon replace Tiberius as emperor. His words were overheard by the driver of the chariot who later reported it to Tiberius. Soon Agrippa was languishing in jail.

Josephus says that while he was in bonds Agrippa received words of encouragement from a fellow convict who prophesied that his bad fortune would not continue for long, and he would soon rise to hold a great position. Josephus also claims that this man had a sinister omen for Agrippa, too. He indicated an owl in the tree nearby and warned that when Agrippa saw it again, it would be a sign that his death would follow five days later.

In line with the prophecy Agrippa was not in prison for long, for Tiberius soon died and was replaced as emperor by Agrippa's friend Caligula. The new emperor ensured that Agrippa was not only released but honoured. He gave him the title king and made him ruler over the land that used to belong to Agrippa's uncle, Herod Philip. Agrippa also gained

Antipas' territory due to the plotting we learned about earlier
(see the section on Antipas), which led to his brother-in-law
being deposed. Caligula further honoured Agrippa by presenting
his friend with a gold chain equal in weight to the iron chains
that had held him in prison.

Agrippa's good fortune continued under the next emperor,
Claudius, who added Judaea and Samaria to his territory,
making him king over a kingdom roughly the same size as that
which his grandfather Herod the Great had ruled.[73] Even more
significantly for many of his people, his reign brought an end
to Judaea being directly ruled from Rome by prefects such as
Pontius Pilate. For the first time in thirty-five years they had
a Jewish king again (albeit one who, like his grandfather Herod
the Great, ruled on behalf of Rome).

Agrippa had legitimacy among his people that Herod the
Great never had, for he had Hasmonean royal blood from
his father Aristobulus and his grandmother Mariamme, the son
and wife of Herod the Great. He was, then, a direct descendant
of the Hasmonean Jewish kings who were so beloved by the
nation (see the first section of this chapter). Agrippa was keen
to please the Jews with his piety, with acts such as presenting
the valuable gold chain that Caligula had given him to the
Temple. It is probably for similar reasons that he had James
the disciple killed, in an attempt to crush the new Christian
cult and thereby demonstrate his religious devotion.[74]

However, Agrippa's good fortune did not last more than a few
years. Acts 12:20-23 records that, when he addressed the people
of Tyre and Sidon resplendent in his royal robes, they declared
him to be a god and not a man. Josephus says that Agrippa
was wearing a silver garment which caught the sun's rays and
reflected light in such a striking way that those who saw it were

terrified. Agrippa seems to have enjoyed the adulation and failed to reprimand the pagan crowd for calling him a god. As a result, the Bible tells us, "... an angel of the Lord struck him down, and he was eaten by worms and died". The fact this incident comes in the same chapter as the murder of James and the imprisonment of Peter may imply that Luke, who wrote Acts, saw Agrippa's death as punishment for his treatment of the Church.

In his description of Agrippa's end Josephus offers the additional detail that just before he fell ill, he looked up and saw an owl perched on a rope above his head and realised that his end was near. Five days later he was dead, just as had been prophesied, suffering what many believe to have been a ruptured appendix. According to Josephus he was just fifty-four.

Further tragedy followed for Agrippa's family. His daughter Drusilla is mentioned in Acts 24:24, together with her husband Felix, procurator of Judaea. Felix is mentioned for his role in Paul's trial. Tragically, Drusilla and Felix's son, named after her father Agrippa, perished at Pompeii in the eruption of Mount Vesuvius in AD 79.[76]

Herod Agrippa II, AD 50-92/93 or 100
(referred to in the Bible as Agrippa)
(Acts 25:13-27; Acts 26)

Agrippa's son, also called Agrippa, was just seventeen on his father's death, so the emperor thought him too young to rule his father's vast territory.[77] Devastatingly for the Jews, this meant Judaea, including the capital Jerusalem, went back to being ruled directly by Rome under procurators. Agrippa was only gradually given small areas of jurisdiction, such as part of Galilee, and none of his territories was anywhere near as large as the kingdom his father had ruled over.

We hear about Agrippa II in Acts 25, when he visits the new Judaean procurator Festus at Caesarea. Festus replaced Felix, who was mentioned in our previous section. We are told that Agrippa was accompanied by his sister Bernice and the pair had come to welcome the new governor (Acts 25:13). The relationship between this sister and brother was something of a scandal at the time. Rumours abounded that they were in an incestuous relationship despite Bernice's attempt to stop the rumours by orchestrating a marriage, a union that did not last long. In her fifties she became mistress to Titus, the future emperor who was twenty years younger than her, but they never married. Titus was forced to end the relationship when he became emperor as public opinion was too strongly against it.[78]

On this visit to Caesarea Agrippa was to meet Paul, who had been imprisoned there for over two years after being accused of rejecting the Law of Moses and causing trouble in the Temple. When they had tried to kill him, the Romans had intervened because of the uproar and ended up taking Paul into their custody for his own protection. In turn, both Felix and Festus struggled to know what to do with Paul. They did not want to aggravate the Jews by freeing him, but also felt obliged to protect him because he was not only a Jew but a Roman citizen, which gave him special rights.

When Agrippa visited Caesarea Festus was dealing with a new complication in Paul's situation: the apostle had appealed for his case to be heard by the emperor in Rome rather than a court in Jerusalem, something he was entitled to as a Roman citizen. This left Festus with a dilemma: how could he explain to the emperor what Paul was accused of? The emperor would expect the charges against him to be laid out clearly, but Festus did not understand the Jewish religion and why they had such a problem with Paul. So he asked Agrippa to help him write a report to explain the case to the emperor (Acts 25:26-27). It makes sense that Festus would seek Agrippa's help for, as Paul himself said, Agrippa, being Jewish, was "especially familiar with all the customs and controversies of the Jews" (Acts 26:2-3).

Agrippa heard Paul explain his case and, like Festus, found nothing which concerned him. Indeed, he seems to have enjoyed listening to Paul. He even jested with him about his forceful arguments saying, "Are you so quickly persuading me to become a Christian?" (Acts 26:28).

We hear no more about Agrippa after this in the Bible. Jewish resentment over Roman rule increased, stoked by the disastrous governorship of procurator Florus, who took power a few years after Festus. Josephus says that Agrippa was involved in trying to quell this dissent, begging his fellow Jews not to rebel against the procurator. However, he was unsuccessful; some of the rebels even turned on Agrippa, throwing stones at him, and he was forced from Jerusalem. Even though many of his fellow Jews were in open revolt against Rome, Agrippa remained loyal to the empire, supplying the Romans with archers and cavalry for the ensuing war against his own people, as well as accompanying the Roman military commander and future emperor, Titus, in the last stages of the war.[79] The Romans rewarded Agrippa for his loyalty with more land and he was made praetor of Rome in AD 75.[80] The exact date of his death is uncertain.

Agrippa II was the last of the Herodian dynasty. These rulers had sought to hold together two conflicting worlds: Jewish and Roman. Ultimately this would prove impossible, with devastating consequences for their people. The rebellion Agrippa failed to stop would lead to the decimation of Jerusalem and, according to Josephus, the slaughter of over one million Jews.

It would also leave the Temple, Israel's holiest place and Herod the Great's masterpiece, razed to the ground. Within seventy years of this devastation, the Romans would have built Aelia Capitolina, a pagan city, on Jerusalem's ruins and the Jews would be forbidden from living there.[51] How different world history would have been if the Herodians had been able to win over the hearts and minds of their people!

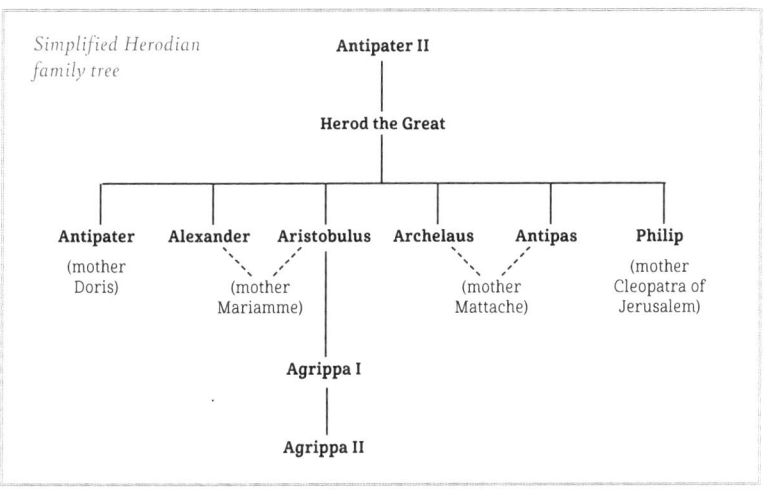

Simplified Herodian family tree

- Antipater II
  - Herod the Great
    - Antipater (mother Doris)
    - Alexander (mother Mariamme)
    - Aristobulus (mother Mariamme)
      - Agrippa I
        - Agrippa II
    - Archelaus (mother Mattache)
    - Antipas (mother Mattache)
    - Philip (mother Cleopatra of Jerusalem)

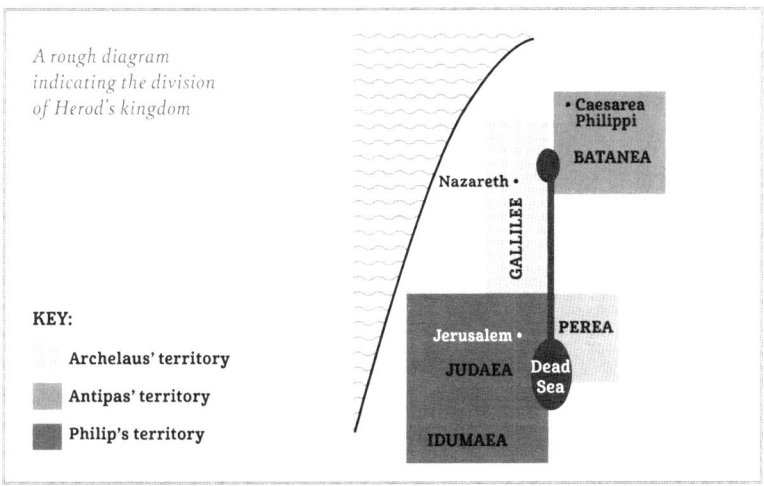

A rough diagram indicating the division of Herod's kingdom

KEY:

- Archelaus' territory
- Antipas' territory
- Philip's territory

Caesarea Philippi
BATANEA
Nazareth
GALILEE
Jerusalem
PEREA
JUDAEA
Dead Sea
IDUMAEA

Anna

Chapter six

Anna

(Luke 2:36-38)

Anna is mentioned early in Luke's Gospel, when Mary and Joseph meet her when they bring the baby Jesus to be presented in the Temple at eight days old. Just before meeting her, they are approached by a man called Simeon, who has received revelation from the Holy Spirit that he will not die before seeing the Messiah (2:25-35). He rejoices at the sight of Jesus believing Christ is, indeed, the one he has been waiting for. Anna then approaches the baby and his family, and we are told that she, too "began to praise God and to speak about the child to all who were looking for the redemption of Jerusalem". Anna is often viewed as a character of little significance in her own right, tagged on to the end of Simeon's story, someone who tells us little more about Christ than Simeon does. If she does, indeed, serve a similar purpose to Simeon and convey a similar message about Jesus, why does Luke mention this woman at all?

One reason may be found in the male-female pairings Luke includes in both his Gospel and its sequel, Acts of the Apostles. Just as Simeon's words about Jesus are followed by a description of Anna, there are many other instances in these books where Luke follows a story about a man with one about a woman. For example, the story of the shepherd who left behind ninety-nine of his sheep to seek out a missing one,

is followed by the parable about the woman who lost one of
ten coins and searched everywhere until she found it (15:3-10).
Similarly, the description of the Angel Gabriel's announcement
to Mary follows directly after Gabriel's visit to Zechariah in
which he was told he would father John the Baptist (1:5-38).
Such male-female pairings are commonly believed to be Luke's
way of showing the Gospel was for both men and women.

Another reason for mentioning Anna alongside Simeon is that,
for a testimony to be taken seriously, it needed to be backed
up by another witness, so Anna's testimony gave Simeon's
legitimacy.[82] If this was indeed the case, it shows how much
Luke valued the witness of a woman.[83] This was unusual in
a time when a woman's testimony was not highly regarded.

Luke, then, clearly wanted his readers to take what both Anna
and Simeon had to say about Jesus very seriously and there
are a number of ways in which he emphasised the reliable nature
of Anna's witness. Firstly, he stressed that she "was of a great age".
However, the Greek text is a bit ambiguous about her actual age.
The NRSV translation says she "lived with her husband seven
years after her marriage, then as a widow to the age of eighty-
four". However, many commentators think Luke intended us to
understand she was even older, and that the Greek really means
she had been a widow for eighty-four years. Most girls were
married very young and it is probable that Anna would have
wed at around fourteen. (This, incidentally, indicates how young
Mary must have been when she became pregnant with Jesus,
for she was still only betrothed.) This reading of the text would
mean that Anna was widowed at the tender age of twenty-one
and lived as a widow for eighty-four years, making her the
grand old age of 105. Interestingly, there was a well-known Jewish
heroine called Judith who reached this exact age. The Book
of Judith which tells her story can be found in any Bible that

contains the Apocrypha. This book says of this ancient character that: "No one spoke ill of her, for she feared God with great devotion" (8:8). It seems likely, then, that Luke wanted his readers to make the connection between Anna and Judith to emphasise that Anna, like this Jewish heroine, was a godly woman.

But Anna's age was not simply important because it connected her to Judith. Old age in general was revered at that time and thought to bring wisdom. This is reflected in Leviticus (19:32*a*), for instance: "You shall rise before the aged, and defer to the old." Similarly, Proverbs (20:29), says, "The glory of youths is their strength, but the beauty of the aged is their grey hair." Anna's age, then, would have added weight to her testimony.

In addition, widows who chose not to remarry but instead dedicated themselves to prayer and God's service seem to have been held in special esteem. This is another way in which Anna was like Judith whom, we are told, many men wanted to marry but who "gave herself to no man all the days of her life after her husband Manasseh died" (Judith 16:22). Luke appears to have had a particular respect and concern for widows, for he included many stories in his Gospel and Acts about them which are not recorded elsewhere – stories such as the one commonly called the "widow's mite", in which Jesus praised a poor widow for giving all she had, even though it was only a tiny amount (21:1-4), and the description of Jesus' encounter with the widow at Nain whose son he raised from the dead (7:11-17).

It has been suggested that Luke's interest in widows such as Anna reflects the growing role they were playing in the Church of his day.[84] Indeed, many people have commented on the similarities between Luke's description of Anna and a list in 1 Timothy (5:3-16), which sets out which widows were

considered eligible for welfare support from the Church.
Widows often needed help if they were without family, but
the Church's limited funds had to be managed well, so this list
sought to prevent widows who already had support from their
families, or were considered likely to misuse the funds, from
taking advantage of the Church's generosity. Interestingly, it
seems that the widows considered worthy to receive support
led lives similar to Anna's. The passage states that a worthy
widow must be over sixty years old, have been married only
once and "be well attested for her good works". It also says that
a "real widow" (without any form of family support) "continues
in supplications and prayers night and day". Such pious widows
were clearly very active, valued members of the Church and
played an important role. Perhaps the example of Anna had
encouraged this way of life among older Christian widows.
Certainly she is likely to have been known by reputation among
the first believers, many of whom would have remembered
seeing her daily in the Temple, and it is not unlikely that they
recalled her fondly and passed on her story to other believers.[85]

Anna's life of prayer and piety is another reason why Luke
probably felt that her testimony about Christ would carry
authority. Luke says, "She never left the temple but worshipped
there with fasting and prayer night and day" (2:37*b*). The Temple
referred to was the Jerusalem Temple, a magnificent building.
Some scholars believe it was possible that Anna could have
lived there, even sleeping on a mat in a corner of the building,
although others think this unlikely.[86] She would, though, have
been at the Temple's daily services, the first of which took
place in the early morning, followed by another at around
three in the afternoon and final prayers at sunset.[87]

The morning and afternoon services would have been very
different from modern church worship, for they involved animal
sacrifice. Animals were not only slaughtered for these services

but throughout the day, as individuals brought livestock to the Temple for private sacrifice. The animals sacrificed in the daily services were lambs. This casts light on an expression John the Baptist used when he called Jesus "the Lamb of God" and, in doing so, was using sacrificial imagery, indicating that Jesus' death on the cross should be seen as a sacrifice (John 1:29, 36).

The lamb sacrificed in the services would have been secured to special posts inside the Temple and was slaughtered, skinned and cut into portions. These were then placed on the altar to be offered as a burnt offering and the lamb's blood, which had been collected in a bowl during its slaughter, was sprinkled on the sides of the altar, as well as emptied out at its base.[88] This will seem distasteful to many, but sacrifice was a common part of most ancient religions and in Israel's case was performed to show gratitude to God or as a way of restoring relationships with the Lord when laws had been broken or people were considered ritually unclean.[89]

Once the sacrifice was upon the altar, singing and prayer began. The Temple officials known as the Levites sang a set psalm for the day accompanied by stringed instruments and at intervals between the singing, two priests would blow a trumpet which acted as a signal for worshippers to prostrate themselves on the floor in prayer.[90]

A visit to the Temple would, then, have been a very sensory experience. Anna spent her days in this stunning building surrounded by people coming and going, hearing the sounds of their chatter, prayers and music, as well as the noise of the animals brought to be sacrificed. And what smells there must have been! There was the aroma of incense which accompanied the main services, the smell of fire and ash as well as burning meat and grain offerings. Yet although Anna was present at every service, she would never have had a great view of the sacrifices being offered at the altar, for as a woman she was not allowed to venture beyond the area known as the Court of the Women.

The altar where sacrifices took place lay in the central part of the Temple complex called the Court of the Priests – an area which, as the name implies, only priests were allowed to enter. This was because it was closest to the very holiest place of all, a building which contained the Holy of Holies where God's presence was believed to dwell. As one drew closer to this part of the Temple, so the purity requirements became more strict.[91] Gentiles were considered the least pure, and could enter the outermost courtyard known as the Court of the Gentiles. Only Jewish men and women were able to go beyond this into the Court of the Women. Even very pious women like Anna were not allowed to go any closer to the Holy of Holies, whereas ritually clean men could continue up sweeping, semi-circular steps through the huge bronze Nicanor Gate into the Court of the Israelites. This area was separated from the Court of the Priests, which contained the altar, by a low barrier, so men could get much closer to this holy site and were probably able to lean over the barrier when offering private sacrifices, laying their hands on the animals and confessing their sins before they were slain.[92] Women were excluded from involvement in such rituals and could only see the altar from a distance through the open Nicanor Gate.

Anna may only have been able to go as far as the Court of the Women, but as an older woman at least she could attend the Temple every day. Younger women were forbidden from entering while they were menstruating, because they were seen as ritually unclean. The thinking behind this is hard for us to understand and scholars have differing views about it.

The idea comes from the book of Leviticus (15:16-24), which likens menstruation to the emission of semen in men, as both are forms of genital discharge and were considered to make a person ritually unclean. However, the emission of semen only caused a man to be unclean for an evening, whereas menstruation, presumably because of how long it generally lasts, made a woman unclean for seven days. Anna's age, then, was also significant because it enabled her to be present in the Temple every day, unlike a pre-menopausal woman.

Anna would have spent her time praying in the Court of the Women. This was a large area that could possibly contain up to six thousand people.[93] It had immense lampstands in each corner which young priests would climb up ladders to light. Their light is described as lighting up every courtyard in Jerusalem, for the Temple was high on a hill and the lampstands could be seen above the walls of this roofless court.[94] Jesus was teaching in the Court of the Women during the Festival of Tabernacles when these huge lamps were lit, so these lights may well have inspired him to talk about being "the light of the world".

The Court of the Women was also the site of the Temple treasury, where thirteen collection boxes were housed. Jesus was in this court when he famously watched a poor widow cast her last few coins into one of the boxes (Luke 21:1-4). There was also an open-roofed room in each corner of the Court of the Women, one of which was known as the Chamber of the Leper. This was where anyone deemed by priests to have been healed of a skin disease went to bathe before being readmitted into society.[95]

We are also told that Anna, in her piety, not only prayed in the Temple day and night but fasted regularly. Most Jews would fast on three special days of the year, including the Day of Atonement.[96] Anna, though, clearly fasted more than this and may well have fasted on Mondays and Thursdays too, like the Pharisees, or even more regularly. In the case of the Pharisees, however, Jesus was not convinced about their motives for fasting so much. In his parable about a tax collector and Pharisee (Luke 18:11-12), he suggests that some Pharisees had become overly proud of their frequent fasts and he shows the Pharisee as boastful, praying: "God, I thank you that I am not like other people: thieves, rogues, adulterers, or even like this tax collector. I fast twice a week..."

Anna is also referred to as a prophet which again adds weight to her testimony about the infant Jesus (Luke 2:36). She is reminiscent of female prophets of the Old Testament like Deborah. However, there is greater significance to Anna being a prophet. It was commonly believed that prophecy had ceased; that in the centuries after the last Old Testament prophets God stopped speaking to the people through prophecy. For instance, the Jewish writings of the Talmud say, "When Haggai, Zechariah and Malachi, the latter prophets, were dead, the Holy Spirit departed Israel".[97] Therefore, characters such as Anna, Zechariah, Simeon and John the Baptist show right at the start of Luke's Gospel that after all these years of silence God's Spirit was moving again. Anna, then, not only points back to the prophets of the past but also forward to a new movement of the Spirit. Her activity can be seen as foreshadowing the pouring out of the Holy Spirit at Pentecost, which Peter declared to be a fulfilment of the Old Testament prophecy of Joel that, "In the last days... God declares... I will pour out my Spirit upon all flesh, and your sons and your daughters shall prophesy" (Acts 2:17).

Anna reveals another link between the Old Testament prophets and Jesus. When she saw the baby Jesus in the Temple, she clearly believed he was the fulfilment of long-standing Jewish expectations, for the passage tells us she spoke "about the child to all who were looking for the redemption of Jerusalem" (Luke 2:38). The phrase "redemption of Jerusalem", together with an expression used in connection with Simeon, "the consolation of Israel", are evocative of the words of the prophet Isaiah (40:1-2; 52:9). Both expressions would have been understood by those who heard them to refer to a messianic figure who was expected to deliver Israel.[98] In Jesus' day, Israel had been conquered by the Romans and so the Jews were ruled by a pagan nation. They longed for some sort of deliverer, a Messiah, someone anointed, chosen by God to save them from their situation.

There were differing ideas, though, about what this messianic figure would be like and how he would deliver Israel. Many believed he would be royal, descended from King David. This went back to a promise found in 2 Samuel (7:11b-16), that God would establish the throne of the Davidic kingdom for ever. David's descendants had not ruled over Israel for centuries, although people still hoped that a Davidic king would return and restore Israel to its former glory. The Gospel writers reflect this, declaring Jesus to be a descendant of David through Joseph (Matthew 1:6-16; Luke 3:23-31). However, they did not share the common belief of many people, that this descendant of David's would be a military leader who would defeat and drive the Romans from Israel.[99] It seems unlikely that Anna did either; she probably had a more peaceable idea of how the Messiah would deliver his people than many, especially as Simeon, with whom Luke closely associates her, said Jesus would be "a light for revelation to the Gentiles", rather than someone who would fight to conquer the Romans (2:32).

Indeed, Jesus himself clearly had no intention of being a warrior figure or worldly king. John's Gospel (6:14-15) tells us that after he had fed the five thousand, he realised the crowd "were about to come and take him by force to make him king" and so he "withdrew again to the mountain by himself". Similarly, Mark's Gospel often shows Jesus instructing his disciples and others not to tell anyone he is the Messiah, probably because those they told would have misunderstood what was meant and would assume he was claiming to be some sort of earthly king (Mark 8:29-30).

Such a misunderstanding is reflected in Jesus' famous rebuke of Peter (Matthew 16:13-23). When Jesus asked his disciples who they thought he was, Peter boldly declared, "You are the Messiah, the Son of the living God." However, when Jesus began to say he would suffer and be killed, Peter was so shocked that he took Jesus to one side and rebuked him saying, "This must never happen to you." To Jesus, though, his suffering and death were central to his messiahship and he rebuked Peter: "Get behind me, Satan!", declaring his ideas human not divine in nature. The concept of a suffering Messiah would continue to be shocking for many Jews as they were expecting their saviour to destroy the Romans, not to be arrested and crucified by them. No wonder Paul would talk about the crucifixion as "a stumbling block to Jews", as under Jewish Law anyone who was hung on a tree (an expression believed to have included crucifixion), was considered cursed by God (Deuteronomy 21:22-23; 1 Corinthians 1:23; Galatians 3:13). This is one reason why the resurrection is so important, for it turned Jesus' death, which appeared to show him as a failure and a fraud, into a victory.

The first Christians, then, believed Jesus was the long-awaited Messiah, but their understanding of the term differed from the common concept of messiahship because they closely linked it to his suffering and death. For Christians Jesus saves and delivers us, not by waging war against our enemies, but through the victory over sin and death that his suffering, crucifixion and resurrection have won.

Anna's belief in Jesus as the Messiah is reflected in another way that is easy to miss. The word "Christ", which we today tend to use as if it were Jesus' surname, is actually the Greek word for "Messiah", and Jesus is referred to as Christ in the very earliest parts of the New Testament, showing that his messiahship was very important to the first Christian believers, most of whom were Jews.

There is an expression that Jesus used frequently in his parables that also relates to the idea of him being the Messiah. He often talked about the kingdom of God/heaven. One Jewish expectation was that the Messiah would establish a temporary kingdom on earth centred upon Jerusalem.[100] The kingdom Jesus spoke about, however, was not a physical territory. As we have seen before, he was not coming to be Israel's king and overthrow the Romans by force. Rather, his kingdom was about God's activity (reign) and can be defined as "God's way of doing things".[101] Through the ministry of Jesus, the Lord's reign had begun to break into the world, changing lives, bringing healing and forgiveness.

There is another interesting detail that Luke gives about Anna which may also be connected to her great desire to see the Messiah. Luke (2:36) says she was "daughter of Phanuel, of the tribe of Asher". Many have wondered why Luke chooses to report this detail and are surprised that Anna would come from this tribe and live in Jerusalem. The tribe of Asher was one of the ten northern tribes of Israel. Anna would be the only Jewish character in the New Testament from one of the northern tribes, whereas all the others were from the tribes of Levi, Judah or Benjamin.[102] The Assyrians had invaded these Israelite territories in 722 BC. Many of the Jewish people there were taken into exile by their conquerors and it is uncertain what became of them. Richard Bauckham believes that some

of the descendants of those northern tribes were living in
Media in Jesus' time and thinks this is where Anna or her family
may have come from. The area Media included what today is
Azerbaijan and Kurdistan. Bauckham thinks that, despite living
a huge distance from Jerusalem, these exiles still viewed the
city as the centre of their faith and had a strong belief that if
they led holy lives, God would enable their people to return
and reunite with the Jews of Judah as the whole people of God
once more, as they had been under King David. He believes
that such hopes had led Anna, or her family, and others who
were awaiting the Messiah and the reuniting of Israel to return
to Jerusalem.[103] Therefore, it may have been Anna's longing for
the Messiah that brought her to Jerusalem and she may have
remained in the Temple because she expected the Messiah
to be revealed there in line with Malachi's prophecy (3:1*b*) that
"the Lord whom you seek will suddenly come to his temple".

Anna's northern background might also indicate a wider
theme in Luke: that Jesus came to seek and save the
lost.[104] Luke has plenty of stories of Jesus reaching out to those
who were believed to be far from God: the prodigal son who
sinned against his father (15:11-32); the tax collector rejected
by society (19:1-10); the woman who had led a sinful life and
anointed Christ (7:36-50). Anna may also show that Jesus was
reaching out to Jews who were "lost" in another kind of way,
who had been forced from the land God had given their
ancestors and were living scattered far from Jerusalem. For
Luke, Jesus came to reach all people and overcome all the
obstacles that lay between them and God: women as well
as men; poor as well as rich; sinners as well as the upright;
Gentiles as well as Jews; and Jews who lived in foreign
countries as well as those in the Holy Land. All, whatever
their backgrounds, could through Christ be united as one
people of God.

We have seen how Anna was an important character in her own right who should not remain in Simeon's shadow. She did not merely repeat Simeon's message that Old Testament prophecies were fulfilled in Jesus but reinforced the authenticity of his witness and added to it. Her devotion to God and longing for the Messiah meant that her opinion would have carried great weight. Indeed, it can be argued that Anna, who never left the Temple, was even more pious than Simeon, who did not spend all his time there.[105] Unlike Simeon (Luke 2:26, 29-30), Anna was not content just to see the Messiah for herself before she died, but wanted to tell others about him. We are told (2:38) that she went "to speak about the child to all who were looking for the redemption of Jerusalem". As Ben Witherington III points out, Jesus' mother Mary may have been the first to be told the good news, but "Anna is the first woman to understand fully and proclaim" it.[106] She may appear in only three verses of the Bible, but she is a woman we should not overlook and her influence should not be underestimated.

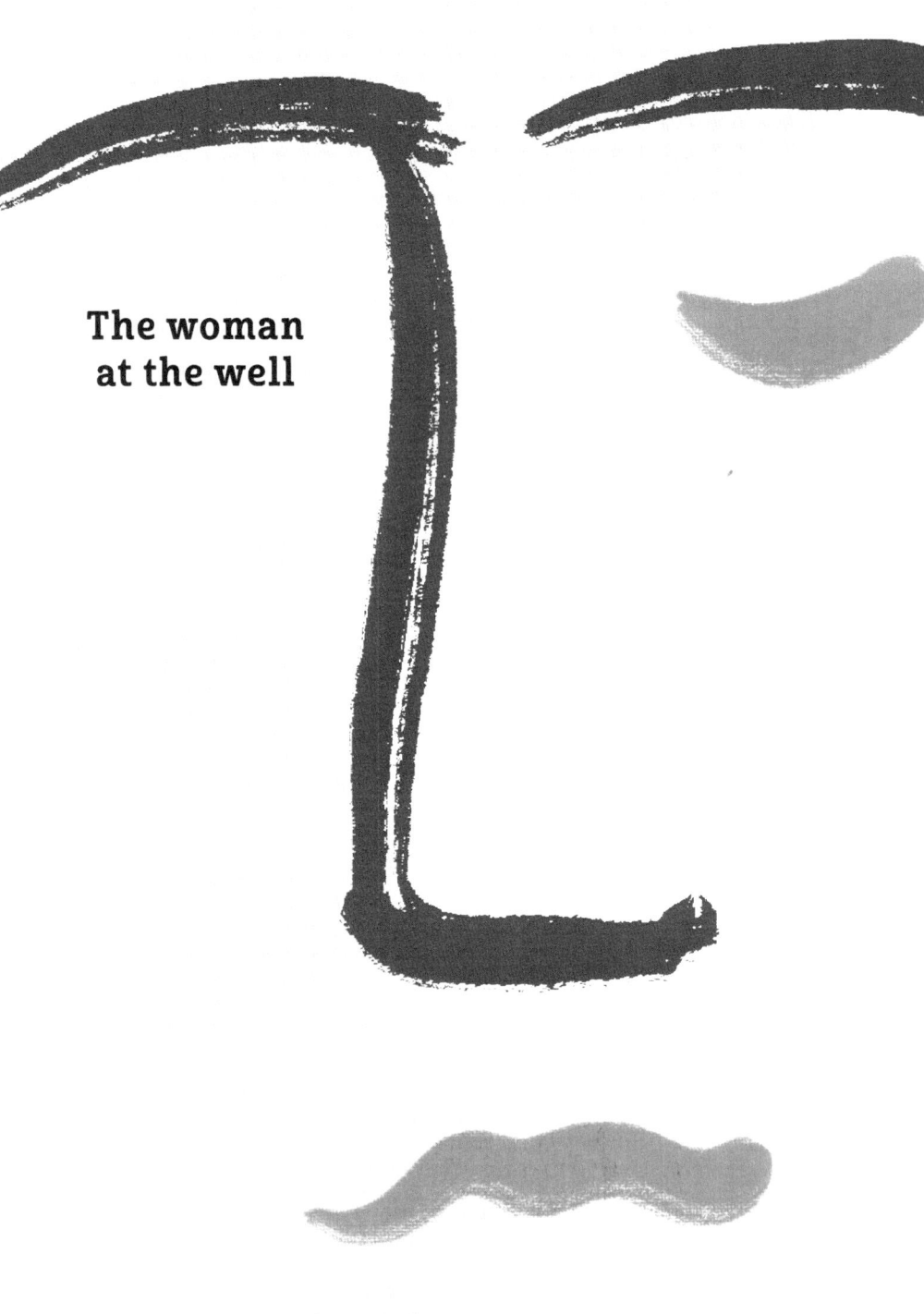

The woman
at the well

The woman at the well

(John 4:1-42)

O ur next character appears in only one chapter of the Bible and we are not even told her name. She is the woman Jesus met at a well in a place known as Sychar. He asked her for a drink and had a deep theological conversation with her. By studying what they talked about, we can discover a lot about the group of people she belonged to, known as the Samaritans. These people appear a number of times in the New Testament including, of course, in Jesus' best-known parable, the story of the good Samaritan.

In John's Gospel we read that Jesus was returning to his home area of Galilee from Judaea by passing through Samaria, a region sandwiched between Galilee in the north and Judaea with its capital, Jerusalem, in the south. In the heat of the midday sun he grew thirsty and tired and rested beside the well which had been dug by the Jewish patriarch Jacob hundreds of years before. It is not surprising that Samaria contained sites important to the Jewish faith, for the Old Testament tells us that this region was once home to a number of Jewish tribes and had been part of one Jewish kingdom under King Saul and then King David. However, after David's son Solomon died in the tenth century BC, the kingdom split, forming Israel in the north, which later came to be associated with the Samaritans, and Judaea in the south.

The Samaritans claimed a common ancestry with the Jews, which was why the Samaritan woman could describe the well as given to her people by "our ancestor Jacob" (4:12).

Even though both the Samaritans and Jews claimed to be descendants of patriarchs like Abraham and Jacob, they were far from a happy family. When the woman arrived at the well, she was shocked to be asked for water by a Jew and said: "How is it that you, a Jew, ask a drink of me, a woman of Samaria?" (4:9). The Gospel writer helpfully explains her bewilderment: "Jews do not share things in common with Samaritans." This is usually understood to mean that most Jews would not drink out of a vessel a Samaritan had used because they believed it would make them ritually unclean.

The relationship between Samaritans and Jews had not been good for many years but had reached a particularly low point by the time of Christ. It seems that in this period many Jews looked down on the Samaritans because they believed they practised a corrupt form of the Jewish faith. Such a view was, for instance, put forward by the first-century Jewish historian Josephus, who justified it by referring to a passage in 2 Kings (17:24-41), which recounts the destruction of the northern kingdom of Israel in 722 or 721 BC by the Assyrian Empire. The passage says that the Assyrians removed the Jews from Israel's northern kingdom and replaced them with people from surrounding countries that were part of their Persian Empire. We are told that although these incomers did eventually come to worship the God of Israel, they continued to serve their "carved images". Such a mishmash of faith was abhorrent to the Jews.

Josephus claimed that the Samaritans were the descendants of these foreign incomers with their syncretic (or combined) religion. He referred to them disparagingly as "Cutheans"

and the descendants of Persians and Medes placed there by
the Assyrian king, Shalmaneser. However, most modern scholars
give Josephus' view little credence, believing it to be a xenophobic
polemic more concerned with portraying the Samaritans as
idolatrous pagans than with historical truth.[107] It is generally
now believed that the 2 Kings passage tells us nothing about the
origins of the Samaritans who existed in New Testament times.
It is thought that the Samaritan community of Jesus' day emerged
considerably later and had no connection to the peoples brought
in by the Assyrian king or their pagan religions.[108]

Today it is generally thought that not all Jews were taken into
exile from the northern kingdom. Rather, it is believed that
a considerable number of Israelites remained there after the
Assyrian conquest.[109] It is suggested that around the fourth
century BC some of these descendants of the old kingdom
of Israel repopulated the Samaritan town of Shechem and
that this is where the Samaritans' origin lies.[110]

Just as the Jews criticised Samaritan religious practices,
the Samaritans held that it was they, not the Jews, who
had preserved the purest form of Judaism. Like the Jews,
they practised the Law of Moses, but they only considered
the first five books of the Bible (the Pentateuch) to be sacred
scripture. Their conscientiousness over keeping the Law of
Moses is reflected in Jesus' story of the good Samaritan, in
which a Samaritan traveller showed compassion for others
by stopping to help a man who had been attacked and left
on the side of the road.

It is difficult to be sure exactly what lay behind the antagonism
between these two peoples, but it was so strong that it led
each to question the purity of the other's faith, despite all they
had in common. However, it is clear that the biggest point

of contention between them was their temples. This was so significant that the woman raised it with Jesus: "Our ancestors worshipped on this mountain, but you say that the place where people must worship is in Jerusalem" (4:20). The mountain she referred to was Mount Gerizim. It was holy to the Samaritans and the site of their temple, which before its destruction had been in direct competition with the Jewish Temple in Jerusalem. Both Jew and Samaritan believed there should be only one sanctuary and thought theirs was the one God had sanctioned. The Samaritans had consulted the book of Genesis and held that the temple should be on Mount Gerizim because it overlooked Shechem where Abraham built an altar when he came into the promised land (Genesis 12:6-7), whereas the Jews looked outside the Pentateuch to the words of David, who wanted to build a temple in Jerusalem (2 Samuel 7:1-17).[111] This was finally achieved by his son Solomon (1 Kings 6).

Tensions over these two temples and the rival priesthoods associated with them became violent. In 128 BC the Jewish ruler and high priest John Hyrcanus, who was seeking to expand his kingdom, destroyed the Samaritan temple. Clearly this devastating deed could only stoke further animosity between Samaritan and Jew. It is probable that this is what finally convinced the Samaritans that there was no place for them within the Jewish faith and encouraged them to see themselves as a separate sect outside Judaism.[112] And the antagonism over these holy sites was still active in Jesus' time. Josephus tells us that some Samaritans defiled the Jerusalem Temple by scattering human bones about it, an atrocity that happened around AD 6. Following on from that Samaritans were banned from the inner courts of the Temple, being excluded from much of this holy place in the same way that Gentiles were, despite the heritage they shared with the Jews.[113]

Another story in the Bible illustrates their animosity over holy sites. Luke tells us that Jesus was travelling through Samaria on his way to Jerusalem. The people in one of the Samaritan villages they wanted to pass through realised where he was heading and that he had "set his face to go to Jerusalem", so refused him access. Indeed, it was so dangerous for Jews to pass through Samaria that some chose to take a much longer route to Jerusalem, avoiding the region, even though it would take six days instead of three.[114] The reality of this threat is illustrated by an event recorded by Josephus, in which a group of Jewish pilgrims from Galilee were massacred in Samaria.[115]

The disciples did not react well to the Samaritans' refusal to let them pass through the village. James and John asked Jesus if they should call down fire from heaven on the village as a punishment. Jesus clearly did not share their attitude, for we are told he "rebuked them". His tolerance towards the Samaritans must have surprised James and John. And what Jesus had to say to the Samaritan woman about their two competing temples would have surprised her too, for despite being Jewish he did not spend time arguing with her for the supremacy of the Temple in Jerusalem, as she might have expected. Instead, he said: "Woman, believe me, the hour is coming when you will worship the Father neither on this mountain nor in Jerusalem" (John 4:21). He went on to explain that "the hour is coming, and is now here, when the true worshippers will worship the Father in spirit and truth" (4:23). He was indicating that there would no longer be a need for a temple, for true worship would happen through Christ, who would remove the barriers between humanity and God, making it possible for all to draw near and worship God anywhere. Arguments over places of worship would be irrelevant: these things would no longer need to separate Jew and Samaritan, for in Christ these two groups would be able to come together.

The fulfilment of this is described in Acts 1:8. At his ascension, Christ commissioned his disciples to be his "witnesses in Jerusalem, in all Judea and Samaria, and to the ends of the earth". He instructed them, then, to reach out to the Samaritans with the Gospel and we see just this happening in Acts 8. Due to the persecution that broke out after the death of the first Christian martyr, Stephen (see chapter 10), Christians fled Jerusalem and spread out into Samaria (Acts 8:1*b*). One of these was Philip, a colleague of Stephen. He preached to the Samaritans proclaiming Jesus to be the Messiah, the long-awaited saviour. This would not have been a concept new to these people for, like the Jews, they looked forward to the arrival of a Messiah.[116] The Samaritans responded extremely positively to Philip's message (Acts 8:6-8). When the church in Jerusalem heard about this breakthrough, they sent Peter and John to Samaria to check out what was happening, for the spread of the Gospel beyond the Jews to the Samaritans was a highly significant event and they needed to be sure it was a genuine move of God. The apostles were clearly convinced, for they were prepared to lay hands on these Samaritan converts so the Holy Spirit could come upon them (Acts 8:14-17). We are told that they did, indeed, receive the Spirit. This is hugely significant, for in that moment the division between Jew and Samaritan was broken and, rather than religion keeping them apart, faith was reuniting them. It was clear for all to see that God had sent his Holy Spirit down upon these Samaritan converts just as upon the Jewish believers at Pentecost. God, then, had shown beyond all shadow of doubt that Samaritans were of equal value and that the Church should treat them as brothers and sisters in Christ and members of God's family. Just how far the Church had come is reflected in the fact that John, who prayed for the Samaritans to receive the Spirit, was one of those who only a few years earlier wanted to send down fire on a Samaritan village. How things had changed!

Today many who do not realise the significance of this event find the delay between the Samaritans' conversion and their receiving the Spirit odd and come up with various explanations for it. But only when we understand what a momentous and controversial step this was in church history, do we realise why the delay was necessary. It was vital that Philip's work among the Samaritans was shown beyond all doubt to be part of God's plan rather than just the madcap scheme of some independent maverick. Hence it was important that the Samaritan mission was shown to have the full approval of the apostles and that it was they who prayed for these Samaritans to receive the Spirit, so no questions would be asked about the genuineness of the event. The long-standing animosity between Jew and Samaritan meant that many Jewish Christians needed convincing that this was God's will.[117] In addition, the Samaritans had been despised by the Jews for so long they really needed to be sure that they were fully accepted by the Jewish Christians.[118] They needed to be convinced that they were viewed as equals and full members of the Church.

By accepting these Samaritans as their brothers and sisters, Jesus' disciples were following in the footsteps of Christ who, in speaking with the woman at the well, challenged the prejudiced attitude of his day. Indeed, this is not the only time Jesus confronted Jewish attitudes towards Samaritans. His parable of the good Samaritan tackles xenophobia head on. It was told in response to a question by a Jewish expert on the Law of Moses who wanted to hear Jesus' interpretation of the rule in Leviticus (19:18) which says you should "love your neighbour as yourself" (Luke 10:27). Christ shocked the lawyer by responding with a story that had a Samaritan as its hero, rather than the Jewish priest or Levite. The neighbours God wanted the lawyer to love were not simply fellow Jews but also those whom he would have seen as enemies. Jesus' story, then, was one of love overcoming xenophobia and division.

In talking to the woman at the well Jesus was challenging
not only xenophobia but other prejudices too. This is reflected
in the disciples' response when they saw who Jesus was talking
to. We are told "they were astonished that he was speaking
with a woman" (John 4:27). Her gender seems to have been
even more of an issue than her ethnicity. Many scholars argue
that this was because rabbis did not speak to women in public,
for it was considered beneath them. William Barclay says
that some of the Pharisees were called "bruised and bleeding
pharisees" because they would shut their eyes when they saw
a woman, causing them to injure themselves by walking into
walls.[119] A rabbi writing about a century before Christ, declared,
"he who talks much with womankind brings evil upon himself
and neglects the study of the Law and at last will inherit
Gehenna" (hell).[120] Of course, the disciples' discomfort and
shock would only have been intensified by seeing that she
was not only a woman but a Samaritan as well.

There was a further reason most rabbis would have run
a mile from this Samaritan woman: her moral standards.
Jesus challenged her on her lifestyle saying, "you have had
five husbands, and the one you have now is not your husband"
(4:18). Three marriages were considered to be the maximum
acceptable number in the eyes of rabbis, and to make matters
worse it seems she was not married to the man she was currently
living with, which would have been scandalous. It was highly
unusual for a woman to collect water at noon in the heat of
the day, which suggests that this woman had been ostracised
by the other women and only went to the well when nobody
was around.

As we saw in chapter 1, on Zacchaeus, Jesus reached out to
the outcasts of society, those who were avoided and rejected
as sinners, and here again we see him doing the same.

Remarkably, it was to this woman, spurned by others because of her ethnicity, gender and moral standing that he declared himself to be the Messiah (4:26), even though this was something he was usually reticent about. Indeed, it has been claimed that this woman is presented as one of seven key witnesses to Christ in John's Gospel.[121] This Gospel records her acting as a witness right away, leaving her precious water jar and rushing to tell her neighbours, "Come and see a man who told me everything I have ever done" (4:29). We then read that "many Samaritans from that city believed in him because of the woman's testimony" (verse 39). Despite the prejudice she faced and the immoral life she had led, she succeeded in evangelising before even the disciples did.

Eastern tradition claims that this woman continued to be a great witness. These legends say that she was called Photina which means "light" and that she went to preach the Gospel in Carthage, North Africa, where she was imprisoned for three years.[122] It is also claimed that she was martyred like St Peter and St Paul in Nero's persecutions together with her son Victor who was an officer in the Roman army.[123]

Her people, the Samaritans, still exist today, albeit much reduced in number. A 2018 newspaper report puts the population as low as eight hundred.[124] They still regard Mount Gerizim, which today is in the West Bank, as their holy site and observe Passover there each year by sacrificing a herd of sheep. They also maintain their claim to be the descendants of the ancient Israelites and believe they are the ones who have held true to the traditions given by Moses.[125] Today they try to maintain good relationships with both the Jews and Palestinians among whom they live. Indeed, it has been reported that they often act as go-betweens, taking packages for Palestinian businesses through Israeli checkpoints, because Samaritans are not subject to the same checks as Palestinians.[126]

Today's Samaritans co-exist peacefully with both their Jewish and Palestinian neighbours. This is something of which Jesus would certainly have approved. After all, his conversation with their ancient ancestor, the woman at the well, broke down barriers and challenged xenophobia. Inspired by such actions and moved by his Spirit, Jesus' followers went on to reunite Jew and Samaritan within God's family of the Church. Because of such events, St Paul could declare to Christians of many different ethnic backgrounds: "all of you are one in Christ" (Galatians 3:28*b*).

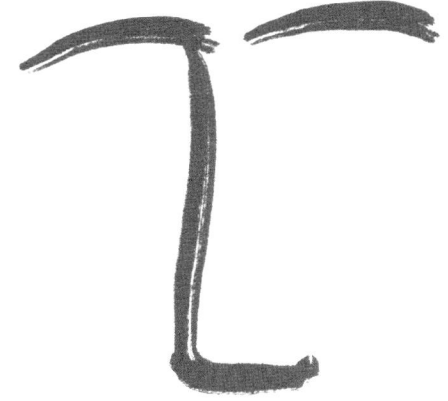

James, the
Lord's brother

James, the Lord's brother

(Matthew 13:54-56; Mark 3:31-32; Acts 1:14;
12:17; 15:1-21; 21:17-26; 1 Corinthians 15:3-7;
Galatians 1:18-19; 2:1-14; James 1-5; Jude 1)

Many people are surprised to discover that Jesus had a brother, even though there are a number of references in the Bible not only to James but to other brothers and sisters too. In Mark 3:32, for instance, as Jesus is teaching, he is told: "Your mother and your brothers and sisters are outside, asking for you." On another occasion when Jesus is in his hometown, people are amazed at his preaching and say to each other, "Is not this the carpenter's son? Is not his mother called Mary? And are not his brothers James and Joseph and Simon and Judas? And are not all his sisters with us?" (Matthew 13:55-56*a*).

There are many other references to James in the New Testament. As well as being mentioned in the Gospels, he also plays an important role in Acts and is mentioned in Paul's letter to the Galatians and 1 Corinthians. We have the letter of James in the New Testament, too, which many scholars believe was written by Jesus' brother, and the letter of Jude, also traditionally held to be written by another of Jesus' brothers. It opens with the line, "Jude, a servant of Jesus Christ and brother of James".

The Gospels suggest that James and his siblings were not followers of Jesus during his lifetime. John 7:5 says of Jesus, "For not even his brothers believed in him." Similarly, Mark 3:21 says that Jesus' family (who we hear in verse 31 included his brothers) arrived at a house where Jesus was teaching "to restrain him, for people were saying, 'He has gone out of his mind.'" These are strong words. Why would they feel this way? Mary was probably a widow by this time as Joseph is not mentioned after the incident when Jesus went to the Temple at the age of twelve. The biblical scholar Ben Witherington explains that in this situation it was the responsibility of the eldest son to keep the family business going and provide for their mother. However, Jesus had left the family home in Nazareth to travel around preaching, leaving James, who is thought to have been the next eldest, to shoulder the load and provide for the family. Did James resent Jesus? Did the family feel shame and embarrassment that Jesus was not fulfilling the traditional role of a good son? Imagine, then, how his brothers must have felt when his ministry ended with his execution as a common criminal. As Witherington implies, this would have sealed the family's shame and may explain why his body was not taken by his kin and buried in a family grave but placed in a tomb belonging to Joseph of Arimathea.[127]

When we move beyond the Gospels and start reading Acts, which is all about the start of the early Church, we read that after Jesus had risen from the dead and ascended to heaven, the disciples went back to Jerusalem where they joined together in prayer "with certain women, including Mary the mother of Jesus, as well as his brothers" (1:14). It appears that something had happened to change Jesus' brothers' views about him. A clue can be found in Paul's first letter to the Corinthians. In chapter 15 Paul sets out what he was told about Christ's resurrection appearances. After Jesus appeared to Peter, the Twelve and five hundred others, "Then he appeared to James" (15:7). It seems likely that James became a believer because of this visit from the risen Christ.

The next time we hear of James in Acts is after Herod Agrippa I arrested Peter and executed another James, the disciple and brother of John. Acts describes how Peter miraculously escaped his chains through the intervention of an angel and returned to the other Christians to inform them of his incredible deliverance. He instructed them to, "Tell this to James and to the believers" (12:6-17). Then we are also informed, somewhat mysteriously, that Peter "left and went to another place". Some believe this indicates that James took up leadership of the Church at this point, as Peter had to flee Jerusalem due to Agrippa's persecution. Others argue that Peter was never the main leader of the Jerusalem church and refer to a quotation from the second-century theologian Clement of Alexandria which states that Peter, together with James and John, chose James, Jesus' brother, to be leader of the Jerusalem church after the ascension of Christ.

Indeed, Paul lists James together with Peter (Cephas) and the disciple John as the main leaders of the early believers, calling them the "pillars" of the Church (Galatians 2:9). As James' name is mentioned first it seems likely that he was the dominant figure in Jerusalem. It is thought James had become the main church leader in the city by around AD 40.[128] James' senior position is reflected, too, in other events that will be discussed later.

The fourth-century church historian Eusebius refers to James as the first to receive the throne of the episcopate in Jerusalem, in other words to be appointed bishop there. However, this is anachronistic terminology as the role of bishop was a later development and it seems likely that James was actually president of the elders in the Jerusalem church.[129] It is also debatable whether he was considered an apostle. Paul's comment in Galatians 1:19, that on a visit to Jerusalem he "did not see any other apostle except James the Lord's brother", could be taken to suggest James was, indeed, an apostle, although the Greek behind this phrase is ambiguous and could also mean that Paul saw no apostles but only James the Lord's brother.[130] James certainly does not seem to have travelled around preaching the Gospel, but unlike others who were called apostles, stayed in Jerusalem and sent out delegates to other churches rather than visiting them.

It is clear that James was the head of the church in Jerusalem, which was the spiritual home of the very first believers and therefore the mother church of Christianity. As the first followers of Christ were also Jews, James came to be seen as the leader of Jewish Christianity. In Galatians 2:9, for instance, Paul says that James, together with Peter and John, agreed that he and Barnabas should go to the Gentiles "and they to the circumcised". We can see a clear delegation of roles early on in church history: James, Peter and John would work among the Jews, and Paul and Barnabas among those who were not Jewish. Indeed, James would not have seen himself as a Christian but as a Jew who had accepted Jesus as the long-awaited Jewish Messiah.[131] For Jews like James, Peter and John, Jesus was the fulfilment of the promises found in their Jewish scriptures (the Christian Old Testament). They would not have foreseen that their faith would eventually end up being considered a religion distinct from Judaism.

It was his position as leader of Jewish Christianity that made James a crucial figure in the biggest dispute faced by the early Church: how to assimilate non-Jewish (Gentile) believers into the Church? As we saw, the first Christians including all twelve apostles were Jewish. Interestingly it appears that this included a significant number of Pharisees (Acts 15:5). These Christian Pharisees were particularly dedicated and serious about keeping the laws found in the first five books of the Bible

(Genesis through to Deuteronomy), commonly referred to
as "the Law" or Torah. They consist of moral laws such as
the Ten Commandments but also regulations on what foods
should and should not be eaten and purification rituals.

These Jewish Christians believed that the Law was a gift
from God and so felt it their duty to ensure it was
observed and not neglected, something they feared might
happen with the influx of Gentiles. They were very keen that
new Gentile believers should be instructed to keep the Law.
More controversially, they also insisted that Gentiles should
be circumcised. For us this may seem a very odd thing to
impose on people who were not Jews, but circumcision,
together with keeping the Law, was central to the Jewish faith
and an important sign of being a member of God's people.

It appears that some of the Jewish Christians were even telling
Gentile believers that, "Unless you are circumcised according
to the custom of Moses, you cannot be saved" (Acts 15:1). This
message was reportedly delivered by a group of Jewish believers
to the largely Gentile church in Antioch, in modern-day Turkey,
where Paul and Barnabas were based. To insist that the salvation
of his Gentile flock depended on circumcision infuriated Paul.
It put into jeopardy his whole missionary work among the
Gentiles and could have led to confusion over his message
that salvation came through faith not the Law. Unsurprisingly,
Acts (15:2) tells us that Paul and Barnabas "had no small
dissension and debate with them".

Things had, then, clearly reached a crisis point and a meeting
was convened to discuss whether Gentile believers should be
circumcised and made to keep the Law. This meeting is referred
to as the Council of Jerusalem and is generally thought to have
taken place around AD 48. Both James and Peter played a leading

role in the meeting and its conclusions, but it was James as leader of the mother church who made the final ruling. He agreed with Paul, saying, "I have reached the decision that we should not trouble those Gentiles who are turning to God" (Acts 15:19). In other words, the same requirements over circumcision and keeping the Law expected of Jews should not be demanded of Gentiles.

Even though James did not require Gentiles to keep all the Law, he did insist that they observed a few aspects of it. He told Gentile believers to abstain "from things polluted by idols and from fornication and from whatever has been strangled and from blood" (Acts 15:20). The comments about abstaining "from things polluted by idols" and "whatever has been strangled and... blood" refer to food regulations. The Jews were forbidden to eat meat sourced from animals that had not been killed in a kosher way by draining the blood, as Leviticus (17:14) warned them not to eat meat with blood in it. Animals that had been strangled would not produce kosher meat. Jews also would not eat meat that had been sacrificed to idols and a lot of meat sold in Gentile marketplaces had been connected to idolatrous practices. Gentile butchers would often sacrifice part of the animals they slaughtered to their pagan deities.[132] Many Jews would feel that eating such meat would involve them in idolatry and cause them to break the commandment not to worship idols (Exodus 20:4-5).

Why was it so important to James that Gentile believers kept Jewish food regulations when these customs were not part of their culture? Eating together was a central aspect of Christian fellowship for these first believers. Acts 2:46, for instance, describes Christians spending time together daily during which "they broke bread at home and ate their food". They brought the meals they would normally eat at home

and shared this food in a fellowship meal which ended with
a primitive form of communion called the Lord's Supper.
However, because Jewish believers followed food regulations
and would be offended by many of the things the Gentiles ate,
there were problems with these two groups eating together,
which affected their fellowship. James' requirements were
designed to enable Jewish and Gentile Christians to eat
together and share fellowship.[134]

Acts 15 portrays James as a supporter of Paul's Gentile mission,
working to bring about the necessary compromises for it to
succeed. However, many think things may not have been as
harmonious between James and Paul as the passage might
suggest. For example, there is an interesting story told in the
first few centuries after Christ (we are unsure of the date
or author) which tells of a violent clash between the two men
which seems to have taken place when Paul (or Saul as he was
known) was still persecuting Christians, before his conversion.
The Recognitions of Clement describes Paul simply as an
enemy who enters the Temple. He is furious to see Jews
turning to Christ and incites violence towards the Christians
before throwing James from the top of the steps in the Temple
and leaving him for dead.[135]

We do not know if there is any truth in this story and,
even if there is, this incident may not have blighted
Paul's relationship with James after Paul had repented of his
persecuting past and become a Christian. However, the Bible
also contains material that has been used to support claims
that there were tensions between the two men. Firstly, in his
letter to the Galatians (2:11-13) Paul describes a clash with
Peter (or Cephas as he calls him, using his Aramaic name).
It appears that Peter had been happy to eat with the Gentile
Christians at Antioch "until certain people came from James".

Paul goes on to say, "But after they came, he drew back and kept himself separate for fear of the circumcision faction." Paul describes challenging Peter over this "hypocrisy" and how "even Barnabas", his close colleague in his mission to the Gentiles, was led astray by these men from James. Clearly, these people were unhappy that a Jewish Christian, especially one in leadership, was eating with Gentile believers.

B ut just because these troublemakers are described as coming "from James" does not mean he agreed with their actions. It could simply mean that they had come from the church in Jerusalem where James was leader. Even if James did have concerns over Paul's Gentile mission, they did not necessarily endure. Scholars disagree about whether Galatians was written before or after the Council of Jerusalem. If this incident occurred before the Council had met, then it is easier to understand why James may have been worried about Jewish and Gentile believers eating together, for that issue had not yet been addressed by the Council. After it had met and James had issued his guidance, it seems unlikely he would still have had concerns over these two groups sharing fellowship meals.

Paul's description of his clash with Peter, then, does not prove that Paul and James were at odds. However, it has been claimed that another part of the Bible provides evidence of conflict between the two men. The letter of James which many believe, as the name suggests, is the work of Jesus' brother, has also been held up as evidence of disharmony between them. James 2:14-26 is commonly understood to directly criticise Paul's doctrine of justification by faith. This is Paul's teaching that we enter a right relationship with God through what God has done rather than what we have achieved. It is summed up in Romans 3:28, in which Paul writes: "we hold that a person is justified by faith apart from works prescribed by the law".

When this is compared to James 2:14, "What good is it... if you say you have faith but do not have works? Can faith save you?", it is easy to see why people have understood James to be challenging Paul.

Even if James were directly addressing what is known as Paul's "doctrine of justification", which is debatable, he was not rejecting it so much as objecting to its misunderstanding and misuse. In other words, he was not opposing Paul, or teaching that we are saved by our good works rather than faith. Rather, he was arguing against the idea that it is possible for someone to have a saving faith which does not affect their behaviour. Indeed, Paul also argued against just such a misunderstanding in Romans 6:1, when he tackled the attitude of some Gentile Christians who believed that God's forgiveness meant they could continue to sin "in order that grace may abound".

Those who suggest James and Paul did not get along need to account for Paul's acknowledgement, in his letter to the Galatians (2:9), that James supported his mission to the Gentiles. Paul says James "recognised the grace that had been given to me" and gave him and Barnabas "the right hand of fellowship, agreeing that we should go to the Gentiles".

While it seems unlikely that there were the strong disagreements that some have claimed took place between James and Paul, it is probable that their different areas of responsibility brought less serious tensions into their relationship. James was concerned primarily with Jewish Christians. He was aware that they would struggle to accept Christianity as the fulfilment of their ancient religion if many of its followers did not think keeping the Law was still important.[136] Paul's primary concern, on the other hand, was for Gentile believers who were likely to be put off following Christ if it involved being forced to adhere to all the rules and regulations of the Jewish Law.

The difficult line James had to tread, between keeping the
Jewish believers on side while supporting Paul's mission
among the Gentiles, came to a head when Paul, prompted
by the Spirit (Acts 19:21; 20:22), visited Jerusalem after his
third missionary journey (21:17*f*), taking the believers there
a collection from his Gentile churches. (Later, when he was
on trial before Felix [24:17], he declared that he had come to
Jerusalem "to bring alms to my nation and to offer sacrifices".)
While Paul and his companions were greeted "warmly" by
the Christians in Jerusalem, and James and the elders "praised
God" when they heard Paul speak about the success of his
ministry among the Gentiles, Acts also reveals that they were
deeply concerned about Paul's presence in the city. Despite
the generous gift Paul had brought, they knew he was deeply
unpopular with many of the Jewish Christians in Jerusalem.
These were the believers whom James and the elders described
as being "zealous for the law". In other words, they were
Jewish Christians who took law-keeping very seriously, and
may even have been converts from among the Pharisees.

What had made these Jewish believers so angry with
Paul? Acts 21 explains that rumours had spread that
Paul had been teaching "all the Jews living among the Gentiles
to forsake Moses", in other words that they no longer needed
to keep the Law. It was also claimed that he had been telling
Jews "not to circumcise their children or observe the customs".
It seems that James did not believe Paul was guilty of this
(verse 24), so what lay behind the rumour? Perhaps they
misunderstood some of Paul's teaching, such as that in
Galatians 5:6 that "in Christ Jesus neither circumcision nor
uncircumcision counts for anything; the only thing that
counts is faith working through love". Jewish Christians may
have concluded that they no longer needed to have their
children circumcised.

The tensions provoked by Paul's visit came at a difficult time
for James: Jerusalem was a particularly volatile place where
anti-Roman nationalism was rife. The Jewish Temple authorities
held power at the behest of their Roman overlords. Therefore,
any group that might in any way inspire public unrest would
be unpopular with the Temple authorities, who would be
concerned that the Romans might clamp down and remove
them from their privileged positions. James and the Jerusalem
church would have been keen, therefore, to show that they were
not a problem that needed suppressing but were law-observant
Jews loyal to the authorities.[137]

James and the elders knew there was a real danger of
violence breaking out among the Jews because of Paul's
visit. So they came up with a plan to try and persuade them
that Paul was a diligent observer of the Law. They asked Paul
to join four Jewish believers in a rite of purification which they
were about to perform at the Temple. The final part of the rite
involved shaving their heads and offering a sacrifice. They
asked Paul not only to take part in this ritual but to pay the
significant costs of the sacrificial offerings for all four men
(Acts 21:23-26). Such a generous gesture would have been
considered particularly pious.[138] Unfortunately James' plan
failed to convince the Jews. Acts 21:27-31 tells us that Jews
from Asia stirred up the crowds against Paul, falsely saying
he had brought Gentiles into the Temple, and he was set upon.
(It was a capital offence for Gentiles to go beyond the Court
of the Gentiles.) Roman soldiers intervened and saved Paul
from the mob and he ended up being taken into their custody
for around two years before being transported to Rome to be
tried by the emperor (Acts 21:31f).

James' efforts may have failed, but this does not detract from
the fact that he had clearly tried to protect Paul. This is further
evidence that their relationship was not as hostile as some have

suggested. Indeed, it can be argued that it was James' support for Paul that led to his own violent death. It seems that James was well respected among the Jews in Jerusalem. He appears to have earned the nickname "James the Just" because of his religious devotion and faithfulness in observing the Law. The second-century writer Hegesippus (AD 110-180) described him as having calloused knees like a camel, due to the amount of time he spent in prayer.[139] However, James' tolerance of Paul would have been controversial and would not have gone down well with the Jewish authorities.

There were other reasons why James became a target despite his undeniable popularity with ordinary Jewish people. According to the historian Eusebius, the Jewish leaders were keen to crush Christianity and were frustrated that Paul had escaped their clutches by being sent to Rome. As leader of the Jerusalem church, James became the next obvious target. In addition, James may further have alienated the powerful chief priests in Jerusalem by criticising how those who were rich treated those who were poor. At this time, the chief priests were depriving the poorer lower-ranking priests of the tithes they relied on to survive and, as a result, some of them had starved to death.[140] If James had been challenging the rich with the sort of uncompromising words used in his epistle (James 5:1): "Come now, you rich people, weep and wail for the miseries that are coming to you," it would not have gone down well with these powerful priests.

James had made some dangerous enemies and when the Roman procurator Festus suddenly died, the High Priest Ananus took advantage of the lack of Roman control in Jerusalem to illegally try James before the Jewish court, the Sanhedrin. The first-century Jewish historian Josephus says that the Sanhedrin found James guilty of breaking the law and, tragically, he was stoned to death.

Josephus' account of James' death is the earliest recorded. Subsequent descriptions include more detail, but it is unclear how many were later elaborations rather than accurate accounts. Eusebius, for instance, describes a tradition which held that James was thrown from the top of the Temple for refusing to denounce Christ and, on surviving the fall, was stoned and beaten to death with a club. Another ancient theologian, Jerome, adds the detail that his legs were broken when he fell from the Temple.

Whatever the exact details, James' murder does not appear to have had the support of most Jews. As we have already seen, James had a reputation of being a pious and holy man and there was an outcry at his murder. Josephus says that most reasonable people believed it to be a miscarriage of justice. Many thought his trial was illegal because the Sanhedrin should not have been called without Roman consent and a number of people complained to King Agrippa II. Some even travelled to meet Festus' replacement as Roman governor, who was on his way to Judaea from Alexandria in Egypt, to raise their concerns. Indeed, so significant was the death of James and so great the sense of injustice that, according to Eusebius, it was believed that the siege and destruction of Jerusalem which followed in AD 70, was God's judgement on the city for it.

Eusebius claimed that James was buried near the Temple where he was martyred and that a monument to him existed there for at least a couple of hundred years. While the monument is no longer there, something else that may be linked with James' death was discovered as recently as 2002, when antiquities collector Oded Golan brought an ossuary box, a stone container used to store the bones of the dead, to André Lemaire, an expert in Semitic scripts. Golan had bought the box years before, but its significance wasn't recognised until Lemaire saw the Aramaic inscription carved into it: "James, son of Joseph, brother of Jesus". Lemaire realised that, if it was genuine, it would be "the first-ever physical link to the historical Jesus of the New Testament".[141] However, the ossuary has divided scholars, with some holding it to be a forgery and others believing it the genuine article.

Despite this recent discovery and James' huge importance in early Christianity, few believers today are aware of his significance. The Church may have historically given little attention to James because in the centuries after his death a variety of non-orthodox movements sought to associate themselves with his memory and gain authority and support for their beliefs in doing so. They presented James in an idealised way, often exaggerating his asceticism. The use of Jesus' brother by such movements may go some way to explain why the letter of James took a long time to be accepted as part of the canon of the New Testament.[142] However, today the value of James' epistle has been generally recognised, with many scholars holding it to be one of the earliest New Testament letters, offering an invaluable insight into early Jewish Christianity in the decades after Christ's death.

James, then, was a very important figure in the early story of the Church. Not only does he remind us of Christianity's Jewish roots, but he was also vital to the Gentile mission. Without this influential leader's willingness to compromise over non-Jews keeping the Law and being circumcised, the spread of Christianity among the Gentiles may have faltered and even petered out altogether. We can thank James that because of his support for the Gentile mission and his wisdom at a crucial point in church history, Christianity was able to become the worldwide faith it is today.

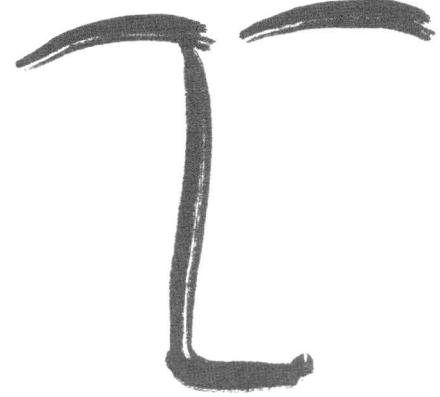

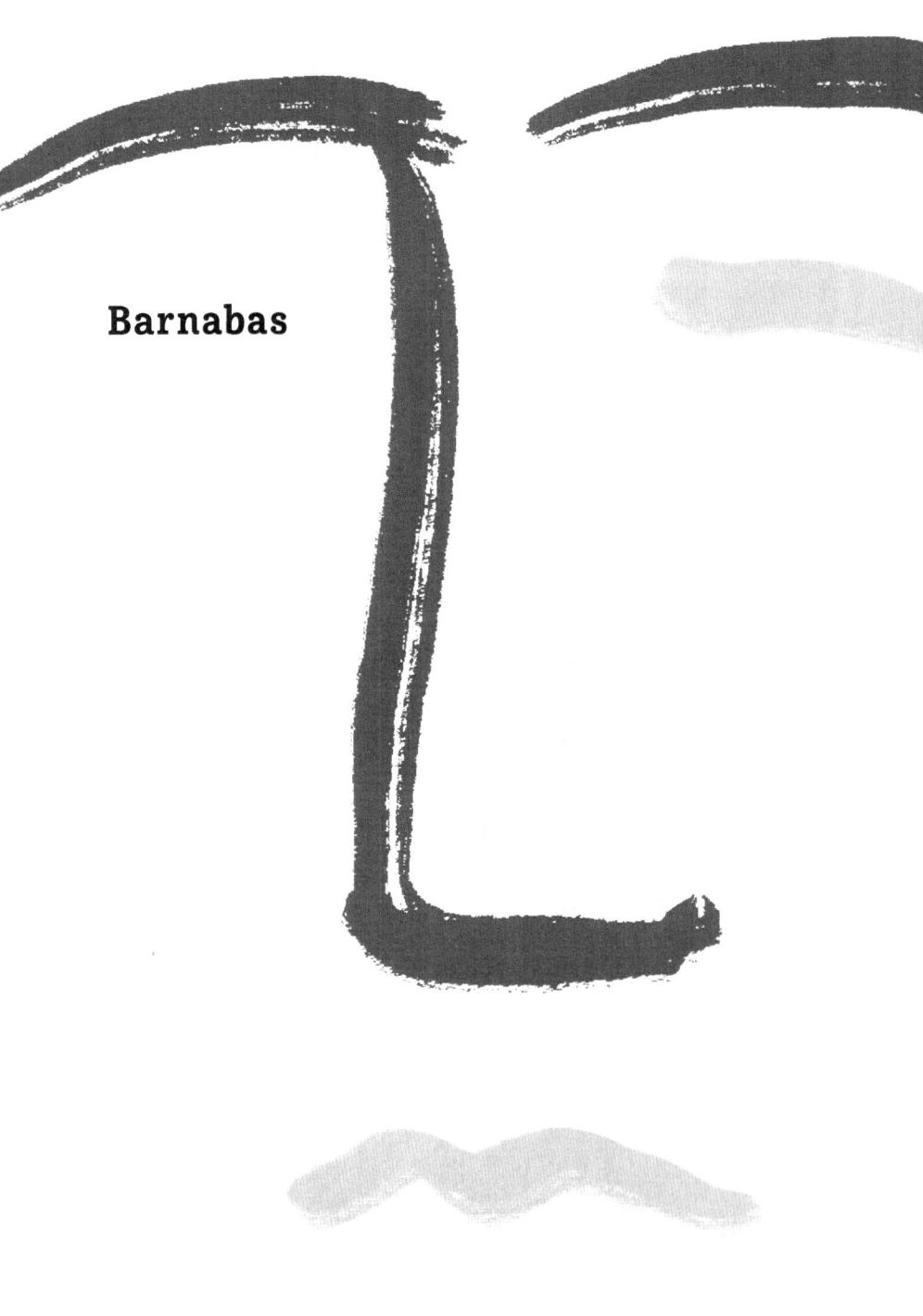

Barnabas

Barnabas

(Acts 4:36-37; 9:26-28; 11:19-30;
12:25-15:4. 35-40; 1 Corinthians 9:5-6;
Galatians 2:6-13; Colossians 4:10)

I f Barnabas is remembered at all, it is usually as little more than Paul's sidekick. This does no justice to the significance of the man and the influence he had on Paul. It is no exaggeration to say that without Barnabas, Paul would never have carried out his ground-breaking missionary work among Gentiles.

His importance is reflected in the number of references to him in several New Testament books. We read of Barnabas in Acts, where he played a vital role in the early Church and he is also mentioned in 1 Corinthians, Galatians and Colossians.

We are introduced to him in Acts 4:36-37 where he is part of the Jerusalem church founded by Jesus' followers shortly after his death. According to Luke, who wrote Acts, one of the remarkable things about this church was the very practical love these first believers showed one another. It appears that a number of these early Christians were poor, for the wealthier among them shared their material resources with those in need (2:44-45). This practical concern for those who were poor seems to have impressed many among the largely Jewish population of Jerusalem, for we are told that "day by day the Lord added to their number those who were being saved" (2:47).

L uke gives us an insight into the godly character which made
Barnabas such a trusted and important leader. He appears
to have been reasonably well off and sold his land, giving the
proceeds to support those in need (Acts 4:37). Luke also shows
that this loving deed was not a one off but typical. Barnabas
was the nickname he was given by the apostles, his real name
being Joseph. The NRSV translates "Barnabas" as "son of
encouragement" (4:36), although some scholars argue that the
name should be translated "son of exhortation" (the phrase "son
of" being indicative of someone's behaviour). The latter would
suggest that Barnabas had prophetic or teaching ability. But in
whatever way we understand the name, Luke clearly wants to
show that Barnabas is held in high regard by the apostles.

A cts 4:36 also tells us that Barnabas was from Cyprus and
that he was a Levite. A Levite was a Jew who belonged
to the tribe of Levi, one of the twelve tribes of Israel. It was
from this tribe that lower-level officials in the Jerusalem Temple
were appointed. However, this does not mean that Barnabas
himself ever took up such a role. Luke probably mentions
Barnabas was of this tribe to show his respectable Jewish
heritage. Indeed, it is likely that despite coming from Cyprus
he would have spoken not only Greek but also Hebrew or
Aramaic just as Jews native to Jerusalem did.[143] Cyprus is
only a few hundred miles from Jerusalem and there had been
a large population of Jews living there for more than two
hundred years. Barnabas' Jewish background together with his
Cypriot roots would be what, in future years, would make him
the perfect bridge-builder between the Jewish believers
in Jerusalem and Gentile Christians further afield.

The Bible does not tell us how Barnabas became a Christian.
However, Clement of Alexandria, writing in the second century,
seems to have believed that Barnabas knew and followed Jesus:

he thought that he was one of the seventy (or seventy-two) disciples Jesus sent out to towns and villages to preach the Gospel (Luke 10:1-17).

We get another clue about Barnabas' relationship with Jesus in 1 Corinthians, when Paul appears to imply that he viewed Barnabas as an apostle, for he compares him and himself to the "other apostles" whom the church supported financially. Paul believed that an apostle was someone who had seen the risen Christ, so this suggests that Barnabas must have been present at one of Jesus' resurrection appearances (9:1-6).[144] He may also have been one of the 120 followers of Jesus mentioned who gathered in Jerusalem after the ascension (Acts 1:15).[145]

The next mention of Barnabas in Acts comes after Paul's conversion. (Paul is referred to by his Jewish name Saul up until Acts 13:13, but for simplicity's sake I will refer to him as Paul when discussing earlier events in Acts.) While he was travelling to Damascus in Syria to arrest followers of Jesus, Paul, a zealous persecutor of Christians, had a dramatic conversion on the road, in which he heard the risen Christ speak to him (9:1-19). After his conversion, the transformed Paul stayed in Damascus preaching about Jesus until a plot to murder him forced him to flee and return to Jerusalem. He hoped to join up with the church there, but unsurprisingly the Christians were not keen to welcome a man who had previously been responsible for "dragging off" followers of Christ and throwing them into prison (8:3). Not only that, but they knew that he had been involved in the death of their beloved Christian brother, Stephen. Stephen was one of seven godly men appointed by the apostles to organise the distribution of food to poor widows (6:1-6). He was stoned to death by an angry mob and the murderers laid their coats at the feet of Paul (7:58), who "approved of their killing" (8:1).

It is no wonder that the Christians in Jerusalem refused to
see Paul because "they were all afraid of him, for they did
not believe that he was a disciple" (9:26).

It is at this point that Barnabas again stands out from the crowd
and demonstrates his gracious nature. Acts 9:27 tells us that:

> *Barnabas took [Paul], brought him to the apostles, and*
> *described for them how on the road he had seen the Lord,*
> *who had spoken to him, and how in Damascus he had spoken*
> *boldly in the name of Jesus.*

Here we see what a vital role Barnabas played in the history
of Christianity. Without his intervention and his willingness to
take a step of faith over Paul, this man may never have been
accepted into the Church; his missionary work may never
have taken place and his letters, which make up such a large
part of the New Testament, may never have been written.
In addition, if Barnabas had not been of such good character,
trusted by the church leaders, it is unlikely that they would
have listened to his assurances about Paul.

Barnabas may have been willing to be Paul's advocate because
he already knew him from before his conversion. The sixth-
century work by Alexander Monachus, *Laudatio Barnabae*,
claims that Barnabas and Paul had both trained under the
Pharisee Gamaliel.[146] Indeed, both men may have been part
of the synagogue that Stephen once attended.[147]

Acts next tells us about Barnabas in connection with the
rapidly expanding church in Antioch. It reports that a
"severe persecution" of Christians broke out after Stephen's death
(8:1). This seems to have focused mostly upon Greek-speaking
Jewish Christians who had been associated with Stephen.[148]

They fled Jerusalem and a number settled in Syrian Antioch, in modern-day Turkey (11:19). There they were responsible for a new wave of evangelism, and took a very radical and important step in reaching out to non-Jews with the Gospel. While many of these exiles spoke only to Jews about Christ, "some men... on coming to Antioch, spoke to the Hellenists also, proclaiming the Lord Jesus" (11:19-20). These Hellenists were likely to be Greek-speaking Gentiles. This was radical because up until this point the Church had been made up virtually exclusively of Jewish believers. Although a few Gentiles had come to the Lord, these Gentiles had links to Judaism (such as the centurion Cornelius in Acts 10) and were already practising aspects of the Jewish faith. But there had been no concerted or deliberate attempt to reach out to the Gentiles before and, had things stayed that way, Christianity would have remained little more than a sect within Judaism. However, the Christians at Antioch changed all this: they actively reached out to Gentiles and "a great number became believers and turned to the Lord" (11:21).

Acts 11:22 tells us that, "News of this came to the ears of the church in Jerusalem, and they sent Barnabas to Antioch." It is clear that the Jerusalem church wanted to find out exactly what was happening in Antioch and ensure this radical new step really was God's will. Again, Barnabas was to play an essential role. The disciples needed someone they trusted, someone they knew would be guided by the Spirit and would make the right judgement. Barnabas, being a Cypriot, shared the same nationality as many of the Christians who were evangelising in Antioch (11:20), making him an excellent mediator between the believers in Antioch and the Jerusalem church. As someone used to mixing with Gentiles he was also more likely to be sympathetic to the idea of a Gentile mission than others from Jerusalem, who were more conservative in their outlook.

So yet again the future of the Gentile mission lay in Barnabas' hands. If he had been uncomfortable with this rapid spread of Christianity to the Gentiles and shared the concerns of many conservative Jewish Christians, that an influx of Gentiles would change the character of their faith and curtail the observance of Jewish practices and keeping the Law, then the Gentile mission could have ended there and then. However, his insight and generous character came to the fore again. Luke tells us that:

> *When he came and saw the grace of God, he rejoiced, and he exhorted them all to remain faithful to the Lord with steadfast devotion; for he was a good man, full of the Holy Spirit and of faith. (Acts 11:23-24a)*

L uke clearly recognised the importance of Barnabas to the Gentile mission and emphasised his godly character. Indeed, Barnabas is the only person Luke calls "good" in the whole of Acts.[149] As F. F. Bruce puts it, Barnabas rejoiced at "the evidence of the free favour of God, unlimited by racial or religious frontiers, extended to all men without distinction."[150]

We next read of Barnabas taking yet another step of faith, in going to Tarsus to bring Paul to Antioch. After he made it possible for Paul to meet the apostles in Jerusalem, Paul spent some time preaching there. However, his life was threatened again and he retreated to his birthplace of Tarsus, only a short boat ride from Antioch. Barnabas was humble enough to realise the task in Antioch was too big for him to manage alone and he needed help. Clearly, he believed Paul had the gifts and background to support him in growing the Church there, because he sought Paul out to assist him. The pair worked together in the city for a year teaching Christians who were largely Gentile. This was hugely significant for Paul: he would never have risen to prominence had he not been given this opportunity by Barnabas. Yet again, Barnabas was prepared to take a risk on someone whom few others would trust. Acts 11:26 reveals that "it was in Antioch that the disciples were first called 'Christians'". This is important, as Christianity was seen as a faith in its own right for the first time, rather than a wing of Judaism. This probably happened in Antioch because there were so many Gentile believers there.

It seems that Barnabas' generous spirit influenced the Christians at Antioch, for when they heard a prophecy about a famine that would affect the church in Jerusalem they organised relief aid which Barnabas and Paul delivered (Acts 11:27-30). Just as Barnabas had been willing to sell his land to help poor Christians in Jerusalem, now the church in Antioch was using its resources to help its mother church. There were close ties between these two churches despite the distance and cultural differences between them. This is not surprising, however, when one remembers that the church in Antioch was founded by refugees from Jerusalem.[151]

After this trip the pair returned to Antioch (Acts 12:25),[152] bringing Barnabas' cousin John Mark, who would join them in the next important stage of the mission to the Gentiles; a missionary journey. Acts 13:1-3 says that a group of teachers and prophets from Antioch gathered in prayer, and while worshipping and fasting the Holy Spirit told them to, "Set apart for me Barnabas and Saul for the work to which I have called them." They then laid hands on them and sent them off. The rich cultural mix of the Antioch church is reflected in those gathered to pray. As well as Barnabas the Cypriot, we are told, there was "Simeon who was called Niger" and "Lucius of Cyrene", both likely to have been North African. In addition, Manaen was "a member of the court of Herod the ruler", alongside Paul, who originated from Tarsus in Cilicia, modern-day Turkey.

This missionary journey was significant, for up until this point the Gospel had reached only places outside Israel where Christians had been forced to flee due to persecution. Now Barnabas and Paul planned a journey which targeted Gentile towns and cities in order to bring them the Gospel. It is also significant that this missionary activity was not initiated by the church in Jerusalem but came from the believers in Antioch. They recognised the Holy Spirit's prompting and set apart Barnabas and Paul for the role. As a result the church in Antioch would grow in significance, effectively becoming the mother church of the Gentile congregations that were founded as a result of this missionary work.[153]

Barnabas' and Paul's journey involved travelling to Cyprus and then on to the cities of Pisidian Antioch (a different Antioch), Iconium, Lystra and Derbe, which were cities in the Roman province of Galatia, modern-day Turkey (Acts 13-14). Barnabas and Paul followed a pattern that Paul would continue in his later missionary journeys: first preaching in the synagogues and then moving on to preach to the Gentiles.

Their mission was a difficult one. They faced hostility throughout their journey from both Jews and Gentiles who stirred up trouble against them. They often had to flee due to threats on their lives from angry mobs and Paul was even stoned and left for dead in Lystra (Acts 13:50; 14:5-6. 19). However, Luke records that despite this opposition, many Gentiles and Jews came to the Lord (13:48-49; 14:1. 21. 27).

An incident during their time in Lystra (Acts 14:8-18) may offer an intriguing insight into Barnabas' physical appearance. Paul had healed a man "crippled from birth". As a result the pagan locals mistook him and Barnabas for Greek gods, calling Barnabas Zeus and Paul Hermes. Merrill C. Tenney says that images of the time "depict Zeus as a tall, dignified figure, wearing a full, curly beard. Hermes was slight, agile, and youthful."[154] This suggests that Barnabas' appearance was more impressive than Paul's. After all, Paul himself refers in one of his letters to his "weak" "bodily presence" (2 Corinthians 10:10). It also implies that Barnabas was the elder of the two and that the Gentiles to whom they preached did not view him as a sidekick to Paul, for Zeus was the chief Greek god who ruled over all the other deities, including Hermes. Even so, the balance of power between the two missionaries appears to have shifted during this journey. Acts implies that Barnabas was the senior figure in the work among the Gentiles both at Antioch and also in the initial stages of his missionary journey with Paul. Up until their departure from Cyprus, Barnabas' name is always mentioned before Paul's which supports this belief (11:30; 12:25; 13:2. 7). After they left Barnabas' native land, though, the Cypriot seems to have fallen somewhat under Paul's shadow, for from that point it is usually Paul who is mentioned first (13:42. 46. 50; 14:1; 15:2. 35).

However, Barnabas still played a vital role and his and Paul's bravery, together with their deep commitment to their new converts, is reflected in their decision to revisit the Galatian cities on their return journey, despite the very real danger of further persecution (Acts 14:21-23). Indeed, they could have taken a much easier route back along the main road which cut through the Taurus mountains and avoided passing through these places all together.[155]

This was to be the last missionary journey that Barnabas and Paul would carry out together. In a very frank passage Luke records that when the pair started to discuss arrangements for another journey, they could not agree whether to take Barnabas' cousin John Mark. He had accompanied their last mission but returned home part way through (Acts 13:13). This clearly had not gone down well with Paul, for when they began making arrangements for the new trip, we are told that:

Barnabas wanted to take with them John called Mark. But Paul decided not to take with them one who had deserted them in Pamphylia and had not accompanied them in the work. The disagreement became so sharp that they parted company. (15:37-39)

It seems likely that Barnabas remained loyal to John Mark because of his family ties to the young man. In addition, as we have seen in the rest of Acts, Barnabas was the kind of man who always gave others a second chance – that was, after all, exactly what he had offered Paul. For Paul, however, their mission to the Gentiles was far too important to put at risk by taking someone along whose commitment was uncertain.

There may have been more to all this than an argument over John Mark, however. An earlier disagreement between Paul and Barnabas may have already tainted their relationship. In his letter to the Galatians Paul refers to an incident in which a group of Jewish Christians from the church in Jerusalem arrived at Antioch when Peter was visiting the church there (Galatians 2:11-14 – note that Peter is referred to as Cephas). When they saw Peter eating with Gentile Christians they were horrified, because it meant he was not following the Jewish food regulations that they thought Jewish Christians should still be keeping. Their reaction may be hard to understand, but they believed that these rules were part of God's revelation to their people and so were still important to follow (for more on this, see the chapter on James). That such a significant leader as Peter would neglect these laws was deeply shocking to them. Peter took on board their criticisms and withdrew from eating with Gentiles. This may have been because he did not want to cause offence or give the impression that he was rejecting his Jewish roots, rather than because he believed there was anything intrinsically wrong with it.

Paul, however, was furious and confronted Peter. He realised that if the will of the Jerusalem believers was imposed on the church in Antioch, then the only way Jewish and Gentile Christians would be able to share fellowship meals, including the Lord's Supper, would be if Gentile believers were required to follow all the Jewish food laws. If these visitors got their way this might have eventually led to Gentile converts being forced to keep every aspect of the Law and imposing these regulations on them would drastically hinder Paul's work among non-Jews.

So it's not difficult to see why Paul would be deeply hurt when Barnabas, his ally and mentor in his work among the Gentiles, followed Peter's example and also stopped eating with non-Jews. Paul's distress is tangible: "even Barnabas was led astray by their hypocrisy", he laments (Galatians 2:13).

It seems likely that it was Barnabas' kindly nature that caused him to follow Peter's example, rather than because he had any desire to impose regulations on the Gentiles. He would have been concerned that his actions were causing distress to his Jewish brethren. He may also have worried that his meals with Gentiles might create problems for the Jewish Christian community in Jerusalem, who were seeking to witness to the Jews around them and demonstrate that following the Christian faith did not mean rejecting their Jewish heritage or abandoning the Law. Barnabas probably also acted out of respect for Peter, whom he would have seen as his superior. However, for Paul important principles were at stake and he was deeply disappointed that his friend could act in a way that might undermine their work among the Gentiles.

It has been suggested that the lack of reference to Barnabas
in Paul's letter to the Galatians may be because Paul was
embarrassed by Barnabas' behaviour. As this letter was written
to the very people the pair had visited on their missionary
journey, indicating that Barnabas was one of the founding
apostles of the churches addressed, we might expect Paul to
mention Barnabas more frequently.[156] However, Barnabas'
actions had put Paul in an awkward spot. In this letter Paul
was arguing against Judaizers, Jewish Christians who were trying
to impose circumcision and law-keeping upon the Gentile
believers in Galatia. Unfortunately, the Judaizers could take
Barnabas' decision to withdraw from sharing meals with Gentiles
as support for their position and use it to undermine Paul.
No wonder he was frustrated and chose not to talk much
about Barnabas in this letter.

Despite the hurt Paul felt over Barnabas' actions in Antioch,
the pair seem to have settled their differences in time
to stand together at the Council of Jerusalem and argue that
Gentile Christians should not be made to keep the Law and
be circumcised. The Council, which was called to discuss
this very issue, is described in my chapter on James.[157] The
argument over John Mark may have stirred up some of the
earlier tensions between the pair and contributed to the
decision not to carry out another missionary journey together.[158]

After they separated, Acts 15:39 tells us that "Barnabas took
Mark with him and sailed away to Cyprus". It seems likely
that he and his cousin returned to strengthen the Christians
in the churches he and Paul had founded in Cyprus. Paul
went back with a new companion, Silas, to check on the
Galatian churches before moving on to preach the Gospel
further afield.

Happily, however, it seems that there was no permanent rift between Paul and Barnabas. Paul still appears to have respected Barnabas: he later mentions him to the church at Corinth, which suggests that he viewed Barnabas as an apostle (1 Corinthians 9:3-6). This also shows that Paul respected Barnabas for funding his missionary activity by means of his own paid work. This they had in common, for Paul also financed his own labours by tent-making (Acts 18:1-3).

The Bible tells us no more about Barnabas, although the Church Father Tertullian, writing in around the third century, claimed that Barnabas wrote the book of Hebrews. This cannot be proven, though, and many have dismissed the idea. However, Barnabas is the only name the early Church links to the letter and his connection to Paul, his Jewish background and his teaching gifts are all strong arguments in his favour.[159]

There are some later legends that claim Barnabas was murdered on his return to Cyprus and buried by John Mark in a cave together with a copy of the Gospel of Matthew. In AD 488 claims were made that the site of his grave had been discovered under a carob tree in a cave northwest of Salamis, Cyprus.[160]

Barnabas was clearly a great man of God. He could discern the leading of God's Spirit, had the courage to step out in faith when others would not, was a skilled mediator between Jew and Gentile and possessed the willingness to reach out beyond his comfort zone with the Gospel. No wonder Luke was full of praise for him. Barnabas was a crucial figure in the history of the Church: someone whose importance is often overlooked. Without him Christianity would not be the cosmopolitan faith it is today: we owe him a great deal.

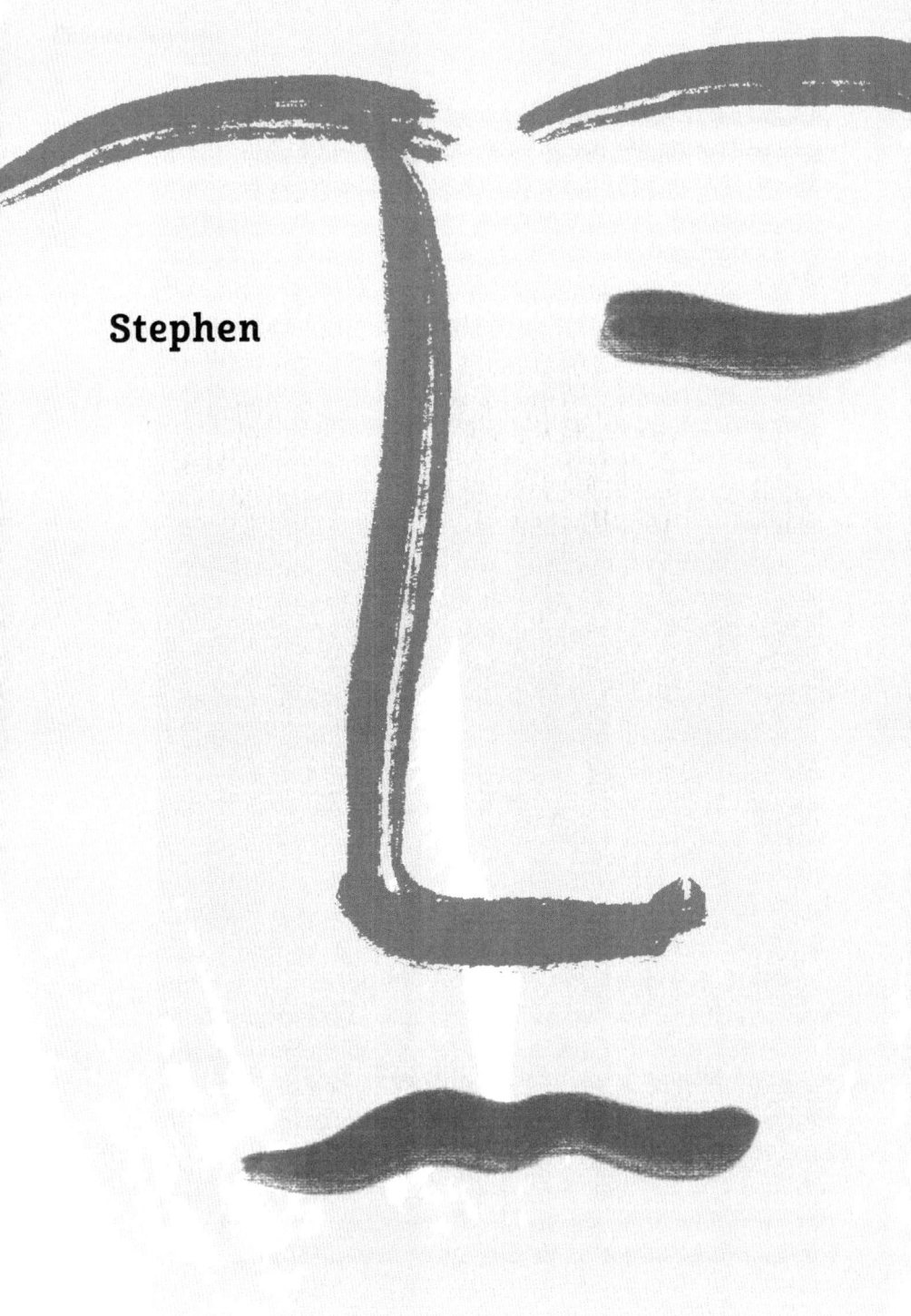

Stephen

Stephen

(Acts 6-8:2; 11:19; 22:20)

Stephen delivers the longest speech in the Book of Acts and, indeed, one of the longest in the whole New Testament. That Luke, who wrote Acts, chose to include this speech in his work implies that he considered Stephen a very important figure in the early Church. In the light of this it is surprising that scholars disagree over exactly why Stephen was significant. So, what can be discovered about this mystery man and why he was so important to Luke?

We first read about Stephen in Acts (6:5) where we are told that he was one of seven men appointed by the apostles to resolve a dispute that had broken out in the early Church. Luke describes this dispute in the following way: "the Hellenists complained against the Hebrews because their widows were being neglected in the daily distribution of food" (6:1). So who were these Hellenists and Hebrews and what were the Hellenists unhappy about?

Hellenist was a word used of Greek speakers. In this context, Luke is using the term to describe Greek-speaking Jewish Christians.[6] These would have been diaspora Jewish believers; Jews who had spent time abroad. Even back in the first century it was common for Jews to live outside Palestine. Some would have been the descendants of Jews forcibly removed from the Holy Land and taken into exile as a result of war, but others had left Israel voluntarily forming colonies in foreign lands.

However, ties with Israel remained strong for these diaspora Jews and many returned. Some came back to Jerusalem during their later years to ensure that they could be buried in the Holy Land.[162] Jewish slaves, too, often returned after completing their period of service once they had been released by their captors.[163] Acts 6:9 offers us evidence of this for it talks of "the synagogue of Freedmen" in Jerusalem which was probably made up of former slaves. Luke's description of the coming of the Holy Spirit at Pentecost also reflects the fact that there were many diaspora Jews living in Jerusalem as well as many who were visiting the city to celebrate the festival, for it talks of "devout Jews from every nation under heaven" in the city (2:5). Some of these diaspora Jews became Christians as a result of witnessing the effects of the Holy Spirit's outpouring. They heard Christ's followers miraculously speaking in many different languages and we are told that three thousand were converted following this miracle and Peter's explanation of it (2:41). It seems likely, then, that a significant number of the Hellenists whom Luke introduces in Acts 6:1 would have been converts of this Pentecost event and would have joined the Church after witnessing it.

The Hebrews, however, that are also mentioned in Acts 6:1 were Jewish Christians who had probably lived their whole lives in Palestine and whose first language was Aramaic.[164] Few of the Hellenists would have been able to converse with them in this language, and while many Hebrews could manage a little Greek, it was not their native tongue. So, although both groups of believers shared a Jewish background and a Christian faith, there was often a language barrier between them.

This would have made it difficult for these different Jewish Christians to worship together. Things were further complicated because the Hellenists used their own Greek translation of scripture, known as the Septuagint, rather than the traditional Hebrew version. It seems likely that the language barrier would have made it necessary for these two groups to meet separately to celebrate the eucharist and, since many continued attending Jewish synagogues as well as Christian meetings, their language differences would have separated them there too, for Hellenist believers are likely to have been members of synagogues in which Greek was spoken.[165] Indeed, Acts 6:9 suggests that Stephen himself was a member of one of these Greek-speaking synagogues, for it describes him debating in the synagogue of the Freemen with Hellenist Jews from Cyrene in North Africa, Alexandria in Egypt and others from Cilicia and Asia which are in modern-day Turkey.[166] It should not surprise us that these Christians kept up links with their Jewish background, for Acts informs us that even the apostles continued attending the ultimate Jewish place of worship, the Temple (3:1).

It appears that the number of Christian converts from both groups of Jews continued to grow rapidly within Jerusalem (Acts 6:1), creating a logistical challenge – how to care for the needy among them, of whom widows were a significant number? It seems that the Hellenist widows were being overlooked in what Luke calls "the daily distribution" and this was causing resentment. So what exactly was this distribution? It probably relates to the early church practice mentioned earlier in Acts in which Christians sold property and land and gave the proceeds to Peter. The resulting funds were distributed to the poor in the church (4:34-35). This may also have involved the daily distribution of food.[167] It appears that as the church increased in numbers it became impossible for the Twelve to manage this practical role without neglecting their other duties. As Acts 6:2 says, the apostles concluded that "It is not right that we should neglect the word of God in order to wait on tables."

But the question remains why only the Hellenist widows were overlooked in this distribution? There has been much speculation on the subject. Were the Hebrew Christians prejudiced in some way against this minority group? Did they view the Hellenists as outsiders or look down on them because of their foreign habits and customs? It seems likely that the language barriers and their membership of different synagogues may have led to problems over practical issues such as the distribution of food.[168]

Others, however, think that too much has been made of the divisions between these groups. Advocates of this view suggest less dramatic reasons for the problems over the daily distribution, such as there being more Hellenist than Hebrew widows in need, so the Hellenists would have been more greatly affected when the distribution was not working well. It is possible that the Hellenist widows were needier because many had left their families when they returned to the Holy Land and had no relatives nearby to support them when their husbands died.[169]

Whatever the causes of the problem, it appears the apostles took the issue seriously and acted quickly to resolve it. They realised they did not have the time to get involved in distributing food and resources themselves because that would lead them to neglect their calling to preach and teach the word of God. So they came up with a solution that was novel for the time. They called together the whole community and told them to select "seven men of good standing, full of the Spirit and of wisdom, whom we may appoint to this task". The apostles, then, did not take sole charge over who was selected as we might expect. Instead they gave over the responsibility to the wider Christian community. It was unusual in a time when those in power tended to suppress dissenting voices that the apostles not only listened to those who were complaining but gave that group the authority to deal with the problem.[170]

The wisdom of this decision is reflected in the names of those selected. All seven men – Stephen, Philip, Prochorus, Nicanor, Timon, Parmenas and Nicolaus – had Greek names and therefore would have come from the Hellenist community who felt neglected. This must have gone some way towards alleviating resentment and helped the Hellenists to trust that their concerns would be addressed. Stephen is listed first probably because he goes on to be central in what follows. However, Philip was also a prominent figure who is described later in Acts (8:26-40) bringing an Ethiopian eunuch to Christ.

It is often held that these seven were the first church deacons, although these roles did not exist at this stage of church history. However, their activities appear to have involved more than simply assisting the poor. Many scholars think that these men became, in effect, the leaders of the Hellenist Christians. Although their responsibilities began with charitable work, their roles developed further. Indeed, after their commissioning by the apostles, Acts does not mention their work among poor people. Instead, we are told that Stephen did "great wonders and signs among the people" and was "full of grace and power". We are also informed that he was involved in debates with unbelieving Hellenists and he appears to have been a gifted communicator, for Luke also tells us that those opposing the Christian message "could not withstand the wisdom and the Spirit with which he spoke".

It was these debates with the Hellenist Jews that got Stephen into trouble. It appears that many of them did not agree with his forceful arguments for Christ and turned to underhand measures to get rid of him. Acts 6:11 tells us that "they secretly instigated some men to say, 'We have heard him speak blasphemous words against Moses and God'". Stephen was then seized and brought before the council or the Sanhedrin, which was the Jewish court. We are told false witnesses were employed who claimed that Stephen:

never stops saying things against this holy place [the Jerusalem Temple] and the law; for we have heard him say that this Jesus of Nazareth will destroy this place and will change the customs that Moses handed on to us. (Acts 6:13-14)

The things Stephen was accused of would have been deeply offensive to most Jews. To criticise the Law and the Temple went right to the heart of Judaism. Jews considered the laws of the first five books of scripture (Genesis through to Deuteronomy) vitally important; after all they had been given to them by God through their prophet Moses. In addition, the Temple in Jerusalem was believed to be the holiest of places. The Temple had been originally built by King Solomon in the tenth century BC, but the version that stood in Stephen's day had been recently constructed by King Herod the Great. Legend had it that it was built on the same site as the Garden of Eden and its presence in Jerusalem was a symbol of Israel's special status as God's chosen people.[7] At the heart of the Temple lay the Holy of Holies where God was believed to dwell. To enter this part of the Temple was to come into God's presence. Consequently, it was considered so holy that only a high priest was allowed to enter that place and then only once a year on the Day of Atonement. The Temple was also the centre of the sacrificial system which was important to the Jews as a means of giving thanks to God and of making amends for sin.

Even though Luke states that the accusations against Stephen came from false witnesses, many scholars think they reveal a lot about Stephen's beliefs. The claim is made that Stephen and the other Hellenist Christians were more radical in their theology than the Hebrew believers, and so differing beliefs and not just different languages separated these two groups. It is argued that the Hellenist Christians, led by Stephen, opposed the Jewish Temple and possibly the Mosaic Law too, just as their accusers claimed. Some have even gone as far as saying they think Stephen believed that the Temple should never have been built at all.[172]

However, the account in Acts does not offer much support for the belief that Stephen was a ferocious critic of the Temple and the Law, or that there were major differences in the theology of Hellenist and Hebrew Christians. Stephen only directly discusses the Temple in a few words towards the end of his speech and it is debatable whether what he says there really is critical of the Temple (Acts 7:44-50). He also describes the Law in positive terms as "living oracles" and, rather than criticising the Jews for observing it, he actually rebukes them for failing to keep it, saying: "You are the ones that received the law as ordained by angels, and yet you have not kept it" (7:38. 53). Indeed, it does seem unlikely that so soon after Jesus' death when the fledgling Christian faith was largely confined to Jerusalem and when the apostles and other Christians were still worshipping regularly in the Temple, Stephen would have completely rejected that place of worship and the Law.

So what, then, could Stephen's speech have been about if it wasn't a radical criticism of the basic tenets of Judaism? One of its purposes was to challenge his accusers over their rejection of Christ by likening them to their ancestors who had rejected prophets such as Moses (Acts 7:25. 35-43). Stephen berates his listeners with the words, "Which of the prophets did your ancestors not persecute? They killed those who foretold the coming of the Righteous One, and now you have become his betrayers and murderers" (7:52).

Rather than criticising the Temple per se, it seems likely that Stephen was warning people not to fall into the error of limiting God to a place even if that place was the Holy Land or the Temple.[173]

If we run through the speech, we can see how this idea is illustrated in the many references he makes to Israelite history. Firstly, he talks about Abraham, the founder of the Jewish faith. The first thing he says was that God appeared to Abraham in Mesopotamia, in other words outside the Holy Land (Acts 7:2). He also points out that although God told him to leave and head for the promised land, Abraham never got to possess it and neither did his immediate descendants. Stephen describes Abraham's descendants as "resident aliens in a country belonging to others, who would enslave them and mistreat them during four hundred years" (7:5-6). Yet even though Abraham did not dwell in the promised land, God was still able to speak to him. For instance, Stephen makes the point that God gave Abraham the rite of circumcision outside the Holy Land (7:8). Circumcision was a sign of God's covenant with the Israelites, a symbol of belonging to the people of God and that fundamental rite was in existence before the Israelites dwelt in the Holy Land and before the existence of the Temple, showing that a relationship with God did not depend upon those things.

Stephen then says that "God was with" Abraham's descendant Joseph even though he, too, was not living in Israel but had been sold into slavery in Egypt (7:9). Similarly he points out that Moses, who delivered the Israelites from that place, was born in Egypt, raised not by his Jewish parents but Pharaoh's daughter, and later heard God's call to him from a burning bush which was not in Israel either but "in the wilderness of Mount Sinai" (7:20-22, 30). Stephen reminds his listeners that God told Moses to take off his sandals before this bush for it was "holy ground" (7:33), again making the point that God's presence was not limited to the Temple or the promised land.

Then in the small section of the speech that directly refers to the Temple, Stephen talks about what preceded that building: "the tent of testimony", a portable tent also known as the tabernacle that the Israelites carried with them in the wilderness (7:44-50). This, too, showed God was with them wherever they went not just the Holy Land. However, those who hold Stephen to have been a critic of the Temple argue that he introduces the tabernacle to make another point: that God preferred it to the Temple and had never even wanted the Israelites to build it. The argument often goes that Stephen was contrasting the two saying the tabernacle was made according to a "pattern" directed by God whereas the Temple was built "by human hands".[174] The implication is that the Temple was a mere human initiative. However, Stephen would have known that the scriptures said the plans for the Temple came from King David, who claimed they were made "at the Lord's direction" (1 Chronicles 28:19).

It seems more likely that rather than completely rejecting the Temple, Stephen was simply saying, as in the rest of his speech, that God is not limited to a place no matter how holy that place was perceived to be. The real contrast in this part of the speech is not between the Temple and the tabernacle but between correct and false views about God's presence. Stephen would not have disagreed that God was in the Temple but that it was wrong to deduce from that that God could *only* ever be there and nowhere else: the Almighty cannot be confined to a building made by human hands. Many also say that Stephen thought the tabernacle avoided such misunderstandings as it was built to be portable, so it could go wherever the Israelites went, reflecting that God was always with them.[175]

To point out that God is not limited to a building or place may seem an obvious statement to make, but Stephen's message was clearly important enough for Luke to devote a significant portion of his book of Acts to it. Why would that be? Acts deals with the spread of Christianity from Jerusalem to Judaea and Samaria and to the ends of the then-known earth (1:8).

For this to happen believers could not be restricted by geographical boundaries but had to be willing to move all around the world in order to spread the Gospel.

If Christianity had stayed tied to Jerusalem, its Temple and its sacrificial system, then it is doubtful the Gospel would have spread widely among the Gentiles, because unless a Gentile was prepared to convert to Judaism and be circumcised, they could not be fully involved in the faith. They would, for instance, have been excluded from the inner courts of the Temple. In fact, there was a wall in the Temple which marked the point beyond which Gentiles were forbidden to go. At regular intervals along this wall were slabs inscribed with the warning that if a Gentile crossed, they faced death.[176] They could not fully participate in the sacrificial system either. They were allowed to offer what were known as votive or voluntary offerings but, unlike Jews, they were forbidden from eating any of the sacrifices. The eating of a sacrifice that had been offered to God symbolised that the participant was in communion with the Almighty, so Gentiles would have felt excluded from a close relationship with God.[177] If, then, the first Jewish Christians had continued to have strong links with the Jerusalem Temple, it is unlikely Christianity would have appealed widely to Gentiles.

There is, however, a further reason why Luke would have wanted his first readers to remember the words of Stephen, for they had a particular relevance to the time they were living in. Most scholars believe that Luke wrote Acts sometime after AD 70, when one traumatic event was still very raw for Luke and his first readers. In AD 70, after the Jews had rebelled against their Roman overlords, the Romans laid siege to Jerusalem. As the city was built on a hill and surrounded by deep valleys, it was not easy to conquer. Indeed, it took the Romans five long months to capture the city, during which time the residents trapped inside endured horrors beyond belief. The Jewish historian, Josephus, an eyewitness of the events, describes starvation so bad that people were forced to eat their shoes and clothing and he claims one woman was so desperate that she ate her own infant.

Eventually the Romans gained control of the city and tragically the Temple was burnt to the ground. An ancient writer Severus claimed that Titus, the Roman military commander who would go on to be emperor, wanted the Temple destroyed because he believed this would lead to the Jewish and Christian religions being completely wiped out.[178] How relevant to these times, then, was Stephen's speech, uttered nearly forty years earlier. How comforted the early Church must have been to read Luke's account and hear what Stephen had declared about God not being limited to Jerusalem and the Temple. It must have encouraged Christians that God was still with them despite the destruction of the Temple and the devastation of Jerusalem. They could also be reassured that Titus' goal of wiping out Christianity was doomed to failure, for their faith did not, as he had assumed, depend on a city or a Temple.

Stephen's thinking on the Temple was probably heavily influenced by Jesus, for Christ had predicted its destruction. In his Gospel Luke records an incident when Jesus was in the Temple and some were admiring "how it was adorned with beautiful stones and gifts dedicated to God". Jesus responded by saying, "the days will come when not one stone will be left upon another; all will be thrown down" (Luke 21:5-6). It appears these words were twisted by Jesus' opponents and used against him at his trial, for one of the accusations made against him was that he had claimed to be "able to destroy the temple of God and to build it in three days" (Matthew 26:61). Of course, predicting the Temple's destruction is not the same as saying he would be the one to destroy it. Interestingly, Stephen was similarly accused at his own trial of speaking "against this holy place" and saying that "Jesus of Nazareth will destroy" it (Acts 6:13-14).

What seems to have sealed Stephen's fate at his trial was a vision. He declared that he could see Jesus in heaven standing at the right hand of God (Acts 7:56). As it is likely that this trial would have been presided over by the same high priest who was involved in Jesus' trial, Caiaphas, and was probably also attended by others who had been involved in condemning Christ too, then it is no surprise that the response to his vision was one of rage. Stephen was effectively saying that Jesus, the man they had condemned and crucified as a common criminal only recently, was now standing in the most prestigious place in heaven, at God's right hand. Not only was this a sharp criticism of their verdict, but to them it would be nothing less than blasphemy: they believed that a crucified man was cursed not blessed (Galatians 3:13). No wonder, then, that we are told "they covered their ears, and with a loud shout all rushed together against him". Indeed, so incensed were people by Stephen's words that his trial appears to have descended into mob violence. We are told that they "dragged him out of the city and began to stone him" (Acts 7:57-58).

While this horrific event was taking place, Stephen prayed for forgiveness for his persecutors, as Jesus had on the cross, crying out in a loud voice, "Lord, do not hold this sin against them" (Acts 7:60). Luke seems to have deliberately drawn parallels between the trials and deaths of Jesus and Stephen. As we have already seen, both were accused of similar things by false witnesses; both also talked about the Son of Man being seated at God's right hand (Luke 22:69); both were innocent (Stephen is described during his trial as having a face like an angel) (Acts 6:15) and both asked God to receive their spirit (Acts 7:59 and Luke 23:46).

This is significant, for Stephen was the first Christian to die for his faith and Luke wanted to emphasise that following Christ would mean walking in Jesus' footsteps and suffering as he had. In his Gospel, Luke described Jesus warning his followers that they would face persecution:

> *When they bring you before the synagogues, the rulers, and the authorities, do not worry about how you are to defend yourselves or what you are to say; for the Holy Spirit will teach you at that very hour what you ought to say. (Luke 12:11-12)*

The inspired words of Stephen's speech were, in Luke's eyes, proof of the truth of Jesus' promise to help the persecuted in their time of need.

Martyrdom was held to be the ultimate form of witness in the ancient world, for if a person was prepared to die for their faith, it showed that they genuinely believed what they were professing. Hence, throughout history, rather than deterring others from turning to Christ, martyrdom inspired the growth of Christianity. Tertullian, the third-century Church Father who lived through a period of persecution himself, famously declared, "We grow up in greater numbers as often as we are cut down by you. The blood of the Christians is their harvest seed."[179] And this seems to have been true with Stephen's death, for even though more Christians were persecuted following his martyrdom, Acts tells us that those who were forced to flee their homes "went from place to place, proclaiming the word" (8:4). They were not deterred by what had happened to Stephen but got involved in spreading Christianity beyond Judaea to Samaria and even further afield to Damascus and Antioch.

Stephen's death is also the first time we read about Saul, or Paul as he became known. We are told that those who stoned Stephen "laid their coats at the feet of the young man named Saul" and that "Saul approved of their killing him" (Acts 7:58; 8:1). After witnessing Stephen's death, Saul began frantically persecuting believers himself. We learn that he entered "house after house; dragging off both men and women" and imprisoning them (8:3). It seems likely that this was not simply because Saul disapproved of Christianity but because Stephen's message had got under his skin. Certainly, many scholars believe we are meant to infer that Stephen was an influence on Saul. It is probable that both attended the same synagogue, for Saul came from Cilicia and Acts 6:9 says that there were Cilicians in the synagogue Stephen disputed in. If so, Saul would probably have heard Stephen talk about Christianity many times, not just at his trial.

The scholar Robert C. Tannehill says that Stephen's influence on Saul is also suggested in the parallels Luke draws between the lives of the two men. For instance, both see Christ in a vision (Stephen at his trial and Saul on the road to Damascus); both suffer for their faith (in Acts, Luke describes Saul being stoned, attacked, imprisoned and tried); Saul, like Stephen, debated with Hellenist Jews and was attacked by them (9:29) and he was seized in the Temple and charged with "teaching everyone everywhere against our people, our law, and this place" (21:28) which are similar charges to those made against Stephen. Indeed, Tannehill points out that Saul starts his speech before his Jewish accusers in Acts 22:1 with exactly the same words Stephen began his speech with at his trial: "Brothers and fathers listen..." (7:2). Saul even refers to Stephen's death and his role in it in this speech saying, "And while the blood of your witness Stephen was shed, I myself was standing by, approving and keeping the coats of those who killed him" (22:20). It seems, then, that Luke meant us to view Stephen as a forerunner and inspiration to Saul and wanted to emphasise that even though Stephen was tragically cut down, God's work continued through Saul.[180]

A cts tells us that Stephen was buried by "devout men" who "made loud lamentation over him" (Luke 8:2). We are not told that these men were followers of Christ and so it seems likely that they were Jews who disapproved of the stoning of Stephen.[181] This is significant because it shows that not all Jews rejected Stephen's message and that some may have had questions over the validity and result of the trial.

There is a tradition that Stephen was buried with Nicodemus and Saul's teacher Gamaliel twenty miles outside Jerusalem. It is claimed that their remains were discovered in AD 415 by a monk who had received instructions on where to find the tombs in a vision.[182] The legend goes that as the coffin was opened a sweet smell emanated and the earth shook. It is also claimed that many of the people crowding around the burial site were healed of a variety of illnesses and that Stephen's remains were transported to Jerusalem on 26 December which, of course, has come to be called St Stephen's Day. It seems apt that Stephen, the first Christian martyr, should be remembered the day after we celebrate the birth of the man whom he gave up his life to follow.

John Mark

John Mark

(Acts 12:12. 25; Acts 13:13; 15:36-40; Colossians 4:10;
2 Timothy 4:11; Philemon 23-24; 1 Peter 5:13)

John Mark has been mentioned in passing in my chapter on Barnabas. However, he is a significant character in his own right and deserves a chapter to himself. He appears in the Acts of the Apostles, but it is likely that he is referred to in several other places throughout the New Testament as well. These passages suggest that he was not only known personally to Luke, who wrote Acts and the third Gospel, but that he also helped both Paul and Peter in their ministries. Many also believe that John Mark was responsible for the earliest Gospel.

We first come across John Mark in Acts 12:12 in connection with Peter's miraculous escape from prison. King Herod Agrippa I had ordered Peter's arrest in Jerusalem, but he escaped from his cell through the intervention of an angel (12:6-11). The first thing he did after fleeing his prison cell was to go straight to the house of John Mark's mother Mary where we are told "many had gathered and were praying".

Mary's house must have been pretty large, for not only are we told it could contain "many" but also that it had an "outer gate" which suggests it possessed a courtyard. Luke also tells us she had a maid called Rhoda, another indication that she was well off. He describes Rhoda hearing a knock at the courtyard gate and says she recognised Peter's voice calling from the other side. Comically, she was "so overjoyed" that rather than open the gate to let him in, she rushed back into the house to tell everyone Peter was outside, stranded behind the gate (12:14)! Traditionally it has been claimed that Mary's house was also the site of "the room upstairs" where the disciples gathered after Christ's ascension and the upper room, in which Jesus shared his last supper with the Twelve (Luke 22:12-13; Acts 1:13).

This Acts passage reveals a few interesting things about John Mark. Firstly, he lived in Jerusalem and was from a relatively wealthy background. Secondly, from a young age he had contact with the very first members of the Church, such as Peter. He is also referred to as "John whose other name was Mark". This reflects what was a common practice among Jews: using two names. John would have been his Semitic name and Mark his Roman one.[183] Interestingly, even though the house Peter fled to belonged to Mary, she is introduced to us as "Mary, the mother of John whose other name was Mark", suggesting that her son was better known to the early Church than she was.

We next hear about John Mark in Acts 12:25, where we are told that Barnabas and Paul (or Saul as he is referred to here and in other early sections of Acts), returned to Antioch in Syria after a visit to Jerusalem bringing John Mark with them.[184] Paul's missionary partner Barnabas was John Mark's cousin, which probably explains why this young man was chosen to accompany the two evangelists to Antioch (Colossians 4:10). Hence, John Mark is linked to two key stages in the growth of Christianity. He had contact with the first followers of Christ, including Peter. These early believers met in Jerusalem and were, in the main, Jewish Christians. Then, after Christianity had spread beyond the Holy Land to Syria, he became involved with the first church to include Gentile as well as Jewish believers which met in Antioch. And he would witness another stage in the growth of Christianity, too, for he was chosen to take part in Paul's first missionary journey.

Acts 13:5*b* reports that Paul and Barnabas took John Mark on their first mission which began in Cyprus. We are told that "they had John also to assist them". We cannot be sure what this involved, however. He may have helped with practical aspects of the journey or possibly have done some preaching. What is clear is that despite all the great things he'd witnessed in his life, John Mark did not last long in this role. Once they had travelled beyond Cyprus, we are told that John Mark "left them and returned to Jerusalem" (13:13). It becomes apparent later that this was no amicable departure, for Paul was clearly very angry about it, so much so that when Barnabas suggested taking John Mark on their next missionary journey, Paul flatly refused. We are told that the disagreement between the two men over John Mark became "so sharp that they parted company" (15:37-41). It seems that Paul felt John Mark had "deserted them". The Greek behind this is very strong and suggests Paul viewed John Mark's departure as a betrayal virtually on the level of apostasy.[185]

There has been much debate over what could have caused John Mark's change of heart. It has been suggested, for instance, that he got homesick and missed his mother's cooking or that he was afraid about the next stage of the journey which involved trekking over the treacherous Taurus mountains.[186] Whatever the cause, his departure led to a radical change in their missionary plans. Paul chose another partner, Silas, for the journey and Barnabas returned with John Mark to Cyprus, presumably to revisit the churches they had established there.

So was John Mark simply someone who did not live up to the opportunities and experiences he'd been given – a spoilt rich boy who could not manage the sacrifice involved in following Christ? That conclusion might be justified were it not for later references to a Mark in the New Testament which most scholars believe describe the same character. These offer us hope that he managed to turn his life around. The first reference (Colossians 4:10-11) gives us an insight into John Mark around twelve years after his split with Paul.[187] Paul probably wrote the letter to the Christians in Colossae from house arrest in Rome. It reveals that John Mark was now with Paul in that city, for he tells them that Mark sends them his greetings and reminds them they had "received instructions" about him and should "welcome him" if he visited Colossae. This implies that the two men were now reconciled, especially as Paul talks warmly of John Mark as one of only three fellow Jews who stayed with him and describes him as a "comfort" to him in his captivity. However, the fact the Colossians needed encouraging to welcome John Mark suggests that even though he had been reconciled to Paul, his past mistakes were well known, and some believers still needed convincing he had changed.

We also hear of John Mark in Paul's letter to Philemon, thought to have been written at the same time as the Colossian letter. In Philemon 24 Paul sends greetings to Philemon from several people including Mark. He calls all these people his "fellow workers" and, interestingly, alongside Mark he also mentions Luke, who most think is the same Luke who wrote the third Gospel and Acts. If so, this shows that when Luke wrote about John Mark in Acts, he was writing about someone that he actually knew. This may even mean that he got his information about the split with Paul and Barnabas directly from John Mark himself.

The second letter to Timothy, which was written later than Colossians and Philemon, suggests that John Mark continued to be on good terms with Paul, for Paul writes to Timothy, "Get Mark and bring him with you, for he is useful in my ministry" (4:11). It appears that by this time Paul had been arrested again and was once more in prison in Rome.[188] He appears sad and alone lamenting that "only Luke is with me". Yet again it seems that Paul is wanting John Mark's presence and support at a difficult time. The man who had once let him down so badly, now seems to have been the person Paul felt he could call on for support and help when there were few others he could rely upon.

B ut Paul was not the only church leader John Mark helped. In 1 Peter 5:13 Peter ends his letter to the churches of Asia Minor with the words, "Your sister church in Babylon, chosen together with you, sends you greetings; and so does my son, Mark." Many believe this Mark is John Mark, and think Peter calls him his son because the apostle had brought him to faith. We have already seen from the book of Acts that Peter knew Mark's mother and presumably her son, so there would have been ample opportunity for Peter to be an influence upon the young John Mark.

Peter probably wrote this letter from Rome because in it he sends greetings from their "sister church in Babylon", who he was presumably with, and Babylon was how Christians often referred to Rome (1 Peter 5:13). This suggests John Mark was with him in Rome which offers further evidence that he had strong ties with that city. Perhaps when Paul asked him to come to Rome, as well as supporting Paul in prison, John Mark also had time to work alongside Peter. It is interesting, too, that Peter passes on greetings from John Mark in this letter which is addressed to churches in Asia Minor (1:1). This suggests that the churches there knew John Mark, implying he had been involved in missionary work in that area himself.

Church tradition may offer us an idea about how John Mark helped Peter. The second-century writer Papias says that someone called Mark acted as Peter's "interpreter" and this has been traditionally held to be John Mark. Scholars are unsure about what this interpreting entailed. It could simply mean that he reported Peter's words and explained them more fully to others.[189] However, John Mark may have played a role more in line with what we think of as an interpreter by translating Peter's teaching for Greek-speaking audiences. Although Peter probably spoke Greek, it was not his first language, so he may have preferred to teach in Aramaic and have his words translated into Greek by John Mark or used him when he wanted his words writing down in that language.[190]

We may be surprised to learn that Peter preached in Rome alongside John Mark because this is not recorded in the Bible. We tend to think of St Paul as the one who travelled widely as a missionary, because we hear all about his work in the New Testament through his letters and the book of Acts which records his missionary journeys. In contrast, the New Testament tells us little about Peter's activities outside Jerusalem. In 1 Corinthians 9:5, we learn that Peter (or Cephas, as he is referred to here) was "accompanied" by his wife on his missionary travels and Galatians 2:11*f* reveals that Peter visited the church in Antioch, in Syria. However, this is all we are told directly about Peter in the New Testament.

George Edmundson makes some interesting suggestions based on these hints we get in the Bible and church tradition. He suggests that Peter may have left the Holy Land to avoid persecution after his escape from prison. Certainly, Acts tells us that after he had informed the believers at John Mark's mother's house of his escape, "he left and went to another place" (12:17*b*). Edmundson argues that at this early point, around AD 42, Peter made a first trip to Rome, possibly to check out and support the growing church there. He argues that by the time Paul wrote his letter to the Romans in AD 57 there was clearly an established church in Rome, even though

Paul had not, as yet, set foot in that city. Indeed, his theory is that Paul held back from visiting Rome because as the apostle writes in Romans, he did not want "to build on someone else's foundations" – in other words, be seen to be interfering in Peter's missionary field.[191]

M ost scholars believe Peter was in Rome between AD 62 and 65, even if they do not agree with Edmundson that he made earlier visits to that city. There are also church traditions that further link John Mark to both Peter and Rome. The second-century Church Father, Clement of Alexandria, claimed that Roman Christians who heard Peter preach asked Mark to write down Peter's teaching for them. Clement believed this was the origin of Mark's Gospel. Papias also supports this by stating that Mark wrote down in his Gospel exactly what Peter remembered and his priority was to ensure he left out nothing he had heard from the apostle.

While we cannot be sure that the Mark whose name has been attached to the earliest Gospel is, indeed, our John Mark, this is what church tradition claims and many scholars believe this is the case because of evidence within the Gospel itself. Mark's Gospel shows, for example, a good knowledge of Jerusalem which was John Mark's home and also contains some passages reminiscent of both Paul's epistles and Peter's first letter.[192] This would fit well with John Mark who, as we have seen, worked with and must have been influenced by both men.

T here is certainly a great deal within Mark's Gospel to support the tradition that someone close to Peter, such as John Mark, wrote it using the apostle as his major source. For instance, in this Gospel we hear Peter's words far more than those of any of the other disciples, and he is the one who is often singled out from the group. For example, at the transfiguration where

Jesus took Peter, James and John up a mountain and they witnessed Jesus' clothes transform into a "dazzling white", we are told that Peter asked to make three dwellings, one for Jesus and the others for Moses and Elijah who had appeared also. However, we are not told anything the other two disciples said on this auspicious occasion (Mark 9:2-6). Similarly, when Jesus found the disciples sleeping after he asked them to stay awake with him during his agony in the Garden of Gethsemane, it is Peter that Jesus singles out, asking, "Could you not keep awake one hour?" (14:37). Peter is mentioned proportionately more in this Gospel than in any of the other ones, as well as being the first and last disciple to be mentioned, which suggests he was significant to the author.[193]

There are also details within Mark's Gospel which appear to have come from an eyewitness such as Peter. For instance, although the Gospel was written in Greek, some of the Aramaic words Jesus spoke have been remembered. For example, when he raised Jairus' daughter from the dead, Mark's Gospel informs us that Jesus said, *"Talitha cumi",* which is translated as "little girl, get up" (5:41). Similarly, there appears to be eyewitness detail in the description of the feeding of the five thousand, for we are told the crowd were asked to sit down on the "green grass", grass of this fresh colour being unusual in Israel's dry climate (6:39).

It is also often noted that Mark's Gospel is blunter about the disciple's weaknesses and failings and the other Gospels try to soften these criticisms. This is further evidence that Peter is the source of these stories, for it seems likely that he would have found it easier to speak honestly about his own shortcomings than someone else would. For instance, in the famous scene where Peter denies Christ three times before the cock crows twice, Peter is challenged by bystanders who believe he is one of Jesus' disciples and Mark tells us that Peter denied this and

"began to curse" and "swore an oath" (14:71). In Luke's version
of this event we are not told about the cursing, presumably
because Luke was reticent to portray the apostle in such a poor
light (22:56-62). Similarly, when the disciples were caught up
in a sudden storm on the Sea of Galilee, Mark records them
saying to Jesus, "Teacher, do you not care that we are perishing?"
whereas Matthew and Luke omit this disrespectful comment
(Mark 4:38; Luke 8:24; Matthew 8:25).

M ark's Gospel is considered to be the earliest Gospel and
is used heavily by both Matthew and Luke, which is why
there are so many similarities between these three Gospels.
The Greek of Mark's Gospel is quite unpolished, more like
spoken than literary Greek, and has a Semitic character to it.[194]
This, too, indicates that it was written by someone like John
Mark who came from Jerusalem and probably spoke Aramaic
as a first language rather than Greek. Indeed, an early Christian
writing, the anti-Marcionite Marcan prologue, suggests that Mark
had the nickname "stumpy-fingered" which may simply have
come about because he had short fingers but could perhaps
refer to the abrupt, inelegant nature of his writing.[195] Yet despite
his unpolished Greek, both Matthew and Luke often reproduce
large parts of Mark's Gospel word for word in their own works.
It seems unlikely that they would have copied so much of Mark
with its uncultured Greek unless they were convinced of its
value. And it seems probable that the reason for the respect they
held for Mark's Gospel was the belief that Peter was its source.

I t is likely that Mark's Gospel was written for the church
in Rome not simply to remember Peter's teaching, but to
encourage the Christians there who were suffering greatly at
the time. This was the age of the infamous Emperor Nero, who
launched a savage attack upon Roman Christians after a terrible
fire destroyed much of the city in AD 64. Many suspected

Nero was behind the fire. There were rumours that he wanted the slums of Rome to be demolished so he could rebuild the city in a way that he found more aesthetically pleasing. When these rumours failed to go away, Nero sought to set up a scapegoat to take the blame for the fire – the new cult, as they were seen, of the Christians. They were blamed for the fire and as a result were executed for public entertainment: "some were crucified, some were sewn up in the skins of animals and hunted down by dogs, some were covered with pitch and set alight to serve as living torches when darkness fell".[196]

How much of this John Mark himself witnessed we do not know. But Mark's Gospel is full of references to suffering and the need to persevere in the face of it. It tells us, for instance, that Jesus faced criticism (2:7, 18; 3:6), shows him warning frequently that he would be handed over, suffer and be killed (8:31; 9:31; 10:33-34), records Christ's warnings that families would be divided as a result of believing in him (1:20; 3:20-21; 13:12-13) and describes him teaching that his followers would face persecution too (4:17; 10:29-30; 13:9-11). Indeed, it is well accepted that both of the apostles John Mark had worked with so closely, his spiritual father, Peter, and the man he had comforted in his captivity, Paul, were executed in the aftermath of Nero's persecutions – Peter by crucifixion and Paul by beheading. How devastating this must have been for John Mark.

Finally, there is one last part of the New Testament that has been connected to him. In Mark's description of Jesus' arrest, we are given one intriguing detail that is not recorded in any of the other Gospels: "A certain young man was following him [Jesus], wearing nothing but a linen cloth. They [the soldiers] caught hold of him, but he left the linen cloth and ran off naked" (14:51-52). Many have wondered if this young man may have been the author of the Gospel himself, for it is difficult to know why this story was included otherwise. If John Mark's mother's house really was where Jesus had his last supper, then Judas and the soldiers may have gone there first, thinking Jesus might still be there before heading to the Garden of Gethsemane to arrest him. John Mark may have heard the soldiers arrive at his home and rushed out of bed, throwing on whatever he could find before running out to warn Jesus.[197] We are told that the garment he threw on was made of linen, which is notable because it was an expensive material and most people would have worn wool.[198] This detail fits well with John Mark who, as we have seen, appears to have come from a well-off background. If this youth was indeed John Mark, then it is probably to him that we owe the record of Jesus' agony in Gethsemane, for the disciples were asleep and could not have witnessed Jesus' desperate prayer for God to "remove this cup" from him and save him from death (14:32-42).

There is a tradition that after Peter's death John Mark went to Alexandria in Egypt where there was a large Jewish population and founded a church there.[199] We do not know anything further about his life after this and we do not know how John Mark died. However, he can be remembered as someone who turned early failure and disgrace around to become a faithful companion to Paul in his time of need and a beloved son to Peter. We, too, owe John Mark a lot, for if he had not written down Peter's recollections of Christ, we would be missing not only the first Gospel, but Matthew's and Luke's too, which depend so heavily upon it. John Mark, then, has ensured that Jesus' teaching, miracles, life and death were recorded for posterity and it is because of him that we are able to read about these two thousand years later.

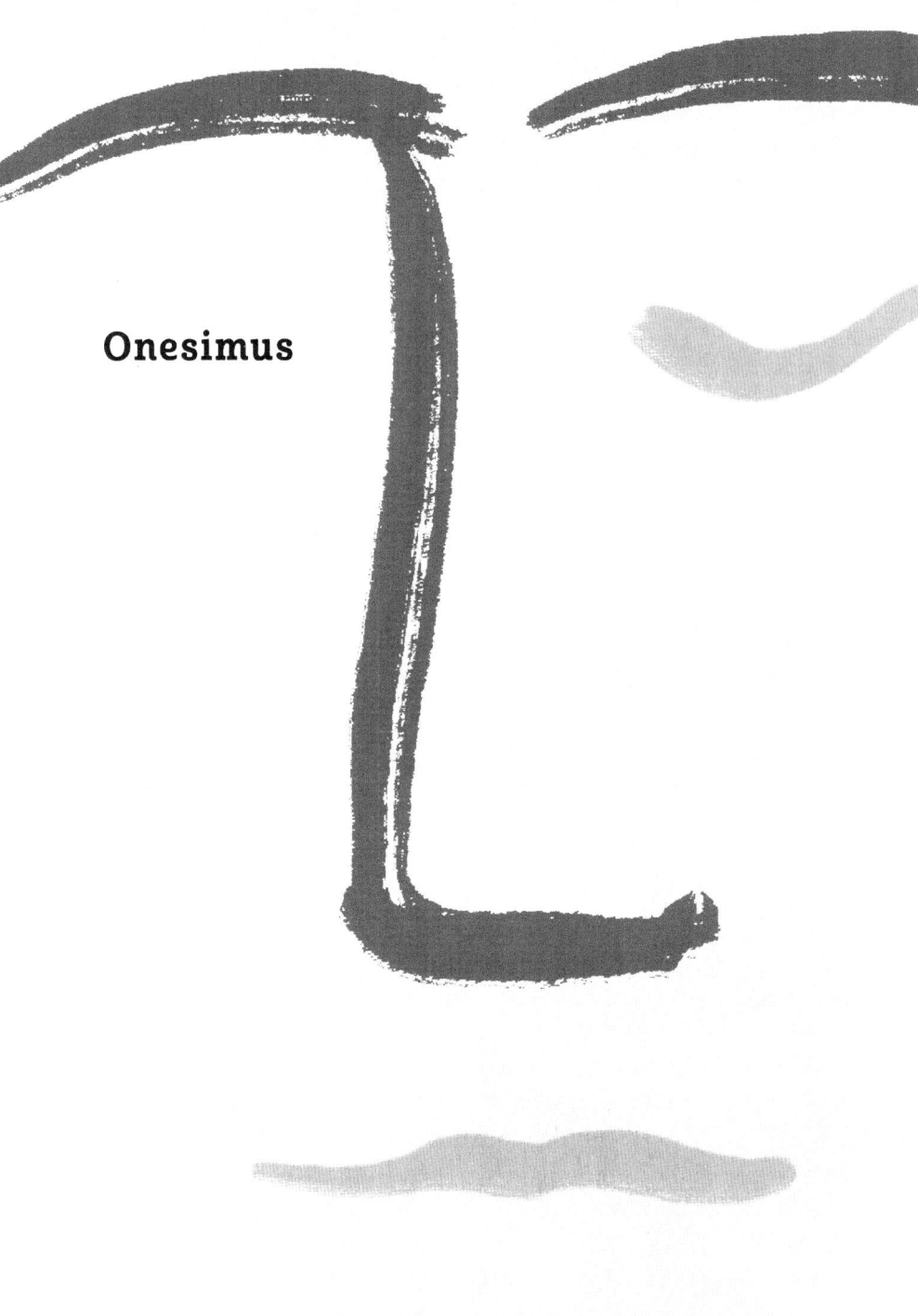

Onesimus

Onesimus

(Philemon)

We learn about Onesimus in Paul's letter to Philemon. This little epistle is the smallest book in the New Testament at only twenty-five verses long. Most believe Onesimus was a slave who had run away from his owner and master Philemon. He later met Paul and became a Christian as a result.

Paul calls Philemon his "dear friend and co-worker" and describes him as having a church in his house (1b-2). It might shock some people to discover that someone who was not only a committed Christian but had worked alongside Paul was a slave owner, but Philemon was not the only Christian slave holder mentioned in the Bible. In Acts, for example, we learn that John Mark's mother Mary had a "maid" called Rhoda who opened the gate for Peter when he escaped from prison (12:13). The Greek word translated as "maid" here is actually "girl", a term used for female slaves.[200] In addition, elsewhere in Acts (16:14-15) we hear about whole households coming to faith, such as the household of Lydia, a wealthy dealer in purple cloth, and it is likely that these households included slaves as well as family members.[201]

This is, perhaps, not so shocking once we realise that owning slaves was common in New Testament times. Around a third of the population of the Roman Empire may have been slaves.

Many owned only a few, but others owned hundreds. Indeed, slavery was such an everyday part of the Roman world that Paul used imagery taken from slavery to help people understand the process of salvation. He talked of being "enslaved to sin" likening sin to a bad slave owner people are powerless to free themselves from (Romans 6:6). He also spoke of Christ who "redeems us" (for example, Romans 3:24; Galatians 4:5; Ephesians 1:7). Slaves were redeemed (set free) when money was paid for their release. Paul used this language of redemption figuratively, to convey the idea that Jesus has bought our freedom, so we are no longer controlled by sin. These were apt images, for the people Paul wrote to in places like Rome were very familiar with slavery and would have immediately understood what he was trying to say.

So where did all these slaves come from? Many were the children of slaves and had been born into slavery. Others were prisoners of war, or those who had sold themselves into slavery through destitution and, most tragically, some had been taken as infants from well-known open-air sites where parents abandoned children they did not want or could not afford – a horrific practice known as exposure.[202]

We tend to think of slavery in terms of the transatlantic slave trade of the sixteenth to nineteenth centuries which involved seizing people from Africa and shipping them as slaves to the Americas. Slavery in the Roman Empire differed in several fundamental ways from this. Firstly, it had nothing to do with race or ethnicity. Onesimus is likely to have had the same skin colour as his master, Philemon. Secondly, slaves performed a wide variety of roles, not just manual labour. While many slaves were domestics or worked in the fields, some were trained and highly skilled – performing, for instance, roles as wide ranging as architect, doctor, artist, hairdresser, weaver or financial manager.[203] They may have performed these roles for their masters directly, or worked for others and given their masters a significant percentage of what they earned. Therefore, being a slave had more to do with a person's status in society than what kind of role they carried out or even how well off they were. Slaves often worked alongside those who were not slaves at the same jobs and may even have been better off financially than some of their free neighbours, who had to pay for their own food, housing and clothing.

However, this does not mean that a slave's life was easy. They were viewed as the property of their masters who were free to treat them as they wished, for slaves had little legal protection. Therefore, their plight depended very much on the character of their owner. Many would beat their slaves if they did not perform as they required, some for very petty reasons. The Roman philosopher Seneca, for instance, said one master whipped his slaves simply because they coughed, sneezed or hiccupped while he was eating. Seneca also expressed his disapproval of whipping or chaining up slaves simply for murmuring under their breath, or a resentful look, suggesting that this, too, was a common practice. And whips in those days were particularly horrific, for they often had pieces of bone or metal attached to them which would tear out chunks of flesh. Slaves were also beaten or prodded with sticks which could cripple, maim or even kill.[204] Some of Jesus' parables reflect this violent treatment. One describes a master who had left a slave in charge of his other slaves while he went away. When he returned and discovered his slave had mistreated the others and been drinking heavily, he gave him "a severe beating" (Luke 12:41-48).

As if such treatment was not bad enough, young female and male slaves were often subjected to sexual abuse by their owners.[205] Again this stemmed from the belief that a slave was their master's property and they, therefore, had the right to treat them as they liked.

If it was not uncommon to treat a slave this way, then would Christian slave owners like Philemon have mistreated their slaves too? The New Testament offers evidence that Christians were taught to treat their slaves reasonably. For instance, in the letter to the church at Colossae, from where Philemon and Onesimus came, Christian slave owners were told to "treat your slaves justly and fairly" (4:1*a*). Similarly, in the epistle to the Ephesians Christian masters are told to "stop threatening" their slaves (6:9). However, the fact that these admonitions had to be made suggests that some, at least, of the slave owners in the Church were still behaving towards their slaves in the same way they had before they were Christians. In addition, these passages do not spell out what it means to treat a slave fairly and views on this would have been very different from what we would consider acceptable today. This may well lead us to the uncomfortable possibility that, for some Christian slave owners, treating a slave justly meant beating them only when they had done something wrong, rather than for a more petty reason.

It is possible that the fear of such punishment may explain why Onesimus ran away. It seems likely that he had done something that would have been considered wrong in his master's eyes, such as stealing from him, for Paul writes to Philemon that if Onesimus "has wronged you in any way, or owes you anything, charge that to my account" (verse 18). Also, Paul makes a pun on Onesimus' name which means "useful" saying the slave was "formerly useless" to Philemon, but that since meeting Paul and coming to faith he was now "useful both to you and to me" (verse 11). This suggests that before his conversion, Onesimus had not been a great asset to Philemon and gives weight to the possibility that he ran away fearing the punishment he expected to receive for some kind of wrongdoing.

The letter to Philemon makes it clear that the runaway ended up with Paul who, as most scholars believe, was in Rome at this point. So how did this come about? We know that Onesimus had fled from Colossae (in modern-day Turkey) where Philemon lived, and had run to Rome, a journey of more than a thousand miles. Onesimus probably headed to Rome because it was easier to go undetected in a big city where half the population were slaves.[206] Paul was under house arrest in that city, so it is unlikely that Onesimus would have been imprisoned in the same place as Paul even if he had been captured. However, it is possible he went to see Paul, as prisoners under house arrest were allowed visitors. But why would Onesimus, who was in hiding, take the risk of revealing himself to Paul? A possible explanation is that Onesimus had been trying to live the life of a fugitive for some time but was struggling. Paul's letter makes it clear that Onesimus had been separated from his master "for a while" (verse 15). It seems that fugitive slaves didn't have many options – they needed food and shelter but had no money. Some joined underground gangs of thieves to survive.[207] Perhaps things had got too tough for Onesimus and he was missing the security of a roof over his head and food, and wanted to return to his master.

But what awaited him could have been even worse than a beating, for he was now no longer simply a badly behaved slave but a runaway. Runaways were treated severely. They were often branded so everyone would know what they had done, making escape even more difficult in the future. Alternatively, runaways could be forced to wear an iron collar around their neck with a warning inscribed on it about their behaviour, and some were even tortured by having the skin burnt off their feet with hot metal plates.[208] Yet if a slave could find someone to mediate between them and their master, someone their master trusted, things could work out more favourably. It seems likely that Philemon had become a Christian through Paul because Paul talks about Philemon owing him "even your own self" (verse 19*b*). Therefore, Onesimus would have known that Paul was someone his master not only respected but was obligated to, because he had led him to Christ. It seems a strong possibility, then, that Onesimus sought out Paul to ask him to appeal to his master on his behalf. He appears to have spent some time with Paul, during which he came to faith and the apostle became attached to his new disciple, for Paul refers to Onesimus as his "child" and calls himself his "father" (verse 10).

Paul was writing to Philemon to ask him to receive Onesimus back without punishment. He appealed to him to welcome the slave "as you would welcome me" (verse 17). He also makes it plain that Onesimus had changed and was now a Christian and so should be welcomed back "no longer as a slave but more than a slave, a beloved brother – especially to me but how much more to you, both in the flesh and in the Lord" (verse 16). To declare a slave to be a brother of their master, and therefore an equal, was very radical. We may wonder how Paul, who said such things and, indeed, elsewhere taught that "there is no longer slave or free... for all of you are one in Christ Jesus" (Galatians 3:28) could send Onesimus back to his master instead of keeping him with him in Rome.

It is important, however, to realise that it was illegal for people to harbour runaway slaves and Paul could have got into severe trouble for doing so. He was already under house arrest awaiting trial and could not afford to get into any more difficulty with the authorities because this could have led to his execution.[209] It is unrealistic to think a man under house arrest could get away with flouting the law and not return a runaway slave. Paul also had to think about the reputation of the Church. If it had got out that a leader of the Christians, a religion that was still in its infancy and viewed with suspicion by many Romans, had been hiding runaways, the Church's reputation, witness and safety would have been at risk.

It is often asked why Paul did not take his belief that Christian slaves and slave masters were brothers and sisters to its logical conclusion and advocate the abolition of slavery. For many it is difficult to reconcile his teaching on equality with other material, traditionally also attributed to him elsewhere in the New Testament, in which slaves are instructed to submit to their masters. For instance, in the letter to the Ephesians (6:5) it says: "Slaves, obey your earthly masters with fear and trembling, in singleness of heart, as you obey Christ." But to criticise Paul for not calling for the abolition of slavery is unfair, for it does not take into account the historical context in which he lived. The Roman Empire was completely dependent on slaves. Without them it would have collapsed. In addition, there was no demand at this time even among slaves themselves for abolition. When there were revolts among slaves, they were never over demands for freedom but for better conditions.[210] This was probably because if slavery had been abolished many slaves would have had no source of income and would have ended up in abject poverty and may well have starved. Finally, we need to remember that Christians were at this stage only a tiny minority with very little power. They could never have won such a fight against the might of the Roman Empire. If Paul had advocated such a revolution, Christianity is unlikely to have survived.

It is also important to realise that freedom from slavery did not lead to what we would consider complete liberation. Freed slaves still had obligations to their former master. For instance, many were expected to continue to work a few days every week or month for their master as hired labourers.[211] Also, if their former master became sick or fell on hard times they were expected to help them, so manumission often did not equate to full liberty.[212] Sadly those who were released never quite attained the status of people who had been born free but were looked upon as ex-slaves (freedmen) who were believed to still need the supervision of their former masters because they were held to be inferior in nature.[213]

Nevertheless, many do believe that in the case of Onesimus, Paul went further than asking Philemon simply to receive him back without punishment. It seems likely that Paul was pushing for him to be freed and, rather than insisting that, once free, he continue to help his former master in Colossae, as an ex-slave would normally be obliged to, Paul hoped that Philemon would be generous and allow Onesimus to return to Rome, so he could continue to help him there instead. Paul did not ask for Onesimus' freedom directly, however, because imposing his wishes upon Philemon could have caused friction and been counter-productive. After all, legally and in the eyes of the culture of the time, Onesimus did belong to Philemon and the universal view would have been that it was the slave owner who had been treated wrongly by his slave and not vice versa. Philemon would be substantially out of pocket through losing a slave and Paul knew that he was more likely to feel animosity towards Onesimus than have any sympathy for a runaway who had caused him so much inconvenience.

Nevertheless, Paul does apply substantial pressure on Philemon in a subtle way. For instance, rather than launch straight into his request, he takes time to win the slave owner over to his cause by starting with an appeal to his better nature. Indeed it is nearly halfway through the letter before he mentions Onesimus and his purpose for writing. He starts by praising Philemon for his "love for all the saints", a tactic designed to make it more difficult for Philemon not to act lovingly towards Onesimus (verses 4-5).

He also writes, "I say nothing about your owing me even your own self", an indirect way of reminding Philemon that he has an obligation to listen and grant Paul's request, because he owes him his very salvation (verse 19). He even tugs on his heart strings by referring to himself as "an old man" and "a prisoner of Christ" (verse 9). In a similar vein, he stresses how useful Onesimus has been while he's been imprisoned for the Gospel and how attached he has become to the slave, calling himself Onesimus' "father" and referring to him as "my own heart" (verses 10-12). He increases this pressure by saying he wants Onesimus to stay with him, "so that he might be of service to me in your place during my imprisonment for the Gospel". In other words, Paul is pointing out that although Philemon hasn't been there to support him in his time of need, through the presence of his slave he can make up for that (verse 13).

Finally, he expresses his confidence that Philemon will do the right thing, making it difficult, of course, for him to do anything else. Indeed, he goes as far as saying: "Confident of your obedience, I am writing to you, knowing that you will do even more than I say" (Philemon 21). This is probably as close as Paul can get to directly asking Philemon to set his slave free. So, although on the surface it might seem that Paul isn't fighting Onesimus' corner because he doesn't ask directly for his release, we can see him using all his powers of persuasion to win Philemon around to his point of view. And it seems probable that Paul was successful, for it is unlikely this letter would have been preserved if his appeals had been rejected and Onesimus had simply been returned and punished.

Indeed, when the prevailing culture is taken into account it becomes clear that many of the instructions in the New Testament about slavery are pretty radical for their time. As we have already seen, Christian masters were instructed to treat their slaves "justly and fairly". They were also warned that

God would hold them accountable for how they had dealt with their slaves – they would not escape judgement because of their higher status on earth, and neither would the plight of the slave be overlooked because of their lowly status. Masters were reminded they, too, have a Master in heaven and that God will show them "no partiality" (Colossians 3:25-4:1).

While it is true that Christian slaves are told to submit to their masters and obey them, the very fact that they are directly addressed in these writings is very unusual and suggests that the Church's attitude towards Christian slaves was more radical than it might appear. That they were addressed directly rather than through their masters and instructed on how to behave shows that Christian slaves were active members of churches who were viewed not as intellectual inferiors or mere appendages of believing masters but as Christians in their own right, as capable of making moral decisions as any believer. Indeed, slaves were instructed to obey not because their master was superior to them but "for the Lord and not for your masters" (Colossians 3:23). The call to obey their owner is probably because at this early stage in Christianity, believers had to take especial care to be good witnesses. They were members of what would have been seen as a new religious cult and they needed to prove they posed no threat to society. If Paul's teaching such as "there is no longer slave or free... for all of you are one in Christ Jesus" had encouraged slaves to argue with their masters or be disobedient, then the Gospel would have been discredited and that would have been a disaster for the progress of Christianity, as the whole movement would have been viewed as seditious and dangerous. Such thinking probably lies behind the teaching in 1 Timothy 6:1: "Let all who are under the yoke of slavery regard their masters as worthy of all honour, so that the name of God and the teaching may not be blasphemed".

H owever, in later centuries the historical context of
such teaching was often ignored, as were the biblical
requirements for masters to treat their slaves well and also
Paul's words on equality and brotherhood. The Bible was even
used to support the institution of slavery and to argue against
the abolition movement. A nineteenth-century Baptist pastor,
Reverend Thornton Stringfellow, felt there was no inconsistency
between advocating slavery and his faith. He even wrote that
Jesus Christ himself upheld the institution of slavery, "as one
that was lawful among men".[214] Similarly, in Solomon Northup's
autobiography *Twelve Years a Slave*, Northup describes one
slave owner reading from the Bible on the sabbath using the
parable in Luke 12 mentioned earlier in this chapter in which
a master beats a slave. He declared this gave him divine
sanction to whip his own slaves![215] Tragically, one former slave
and abolitionist Frederick Douglass wrote:

> *For all slaveholders with whom I have ever met, religious*
> *slaveholders are the worst. I have ever found them the*
> *meanest and basest, the most cruel and cowardly, of all*
> *others. It was my unhappy lot... to belong to a religious*
> *slaveholder... He always managed to have one or more*
> *of his slaves to whip every Monday morning.*[216]

B ut the radical implications of biblical passages such as
Paul's declaration that Philemon and Onesimus were
brothers could not be suppressed for ever. As F. F. Bruce writes,
this letter to Philemon brings us "into an atmosphere in which
the institution could only wilt and die".[217] And, indeed, many
Christians were inspired by scripture to fight slavery. Harriet
Beecher Stow, for instance, wrote the anti-slavery novel *Uncle
Tom's Cabin* as a result of visions she believed came from God.
As the introduction to her novel says:

> *She has brought slavery and the Christianity of the Scripture
> into juxta-position... Doctors in divinity had for a long time
> attempted to dilute both slavery and the Gospel, to render
> them capable of blending... But a woman has come forward,
> has exposed these false prophets.*[218]

And, of course, it was a Christian, William Wilberforce,
who was key in bringing about the abolition of slavery in
the British Empire. He corresponded with the potter Josiah
Wedgwood, who made a famous engraving of a slave in chains
which was used to promote the cause and appeared on very
popular medallions that people wore to show their support
for abolition. This engraving had under it the words, "Am I not
a man and a brother", which is likely to have been inspired by
Paul's declaration that Philemon should now view Onesimus
as his brother.

So what happened to Onesimus? Tradition has it that not only
was he released, but he became Bishop of Ephesus. If this
is so, it may explain why this tiny, very personal letter about a
slave was included in the New Testament. As bishop, Onesimus
may have made sure that the letter that negotiated his freedom
was included in the Pauline epistles that were collected and
edited during his lifetime.[219]

The story of Onesimus reminds us how important it is to
use scripture thoughtfully and to take time to understand
the historical context in which the passages were written.
Paul did not call for the abolition of slavery, but to do that
would, as we've seen, have been inconceivable at the time.
Once we recognise this, it becomes apparent that rather
than being backward in thought, his teaching on slavery
was a radical challenge to the norms of society. He sought
to model change through the Church first, to encourage it

to be a unique community where slaves and masters would come together to worship and love each other as sisters and brothers, demonstrating to the world that all are one in Christ. And it seems likely he succeeded in the case of Onesimus and Philemon. The implications of his teaching that master and slave were brothers were not understood for a long time, but in later years inspired others to fight for the abolition of slavery. How amazed Onesimus would have been if he had known the impact his story would have on the fate of other slaves all around the world, so many centuries later.

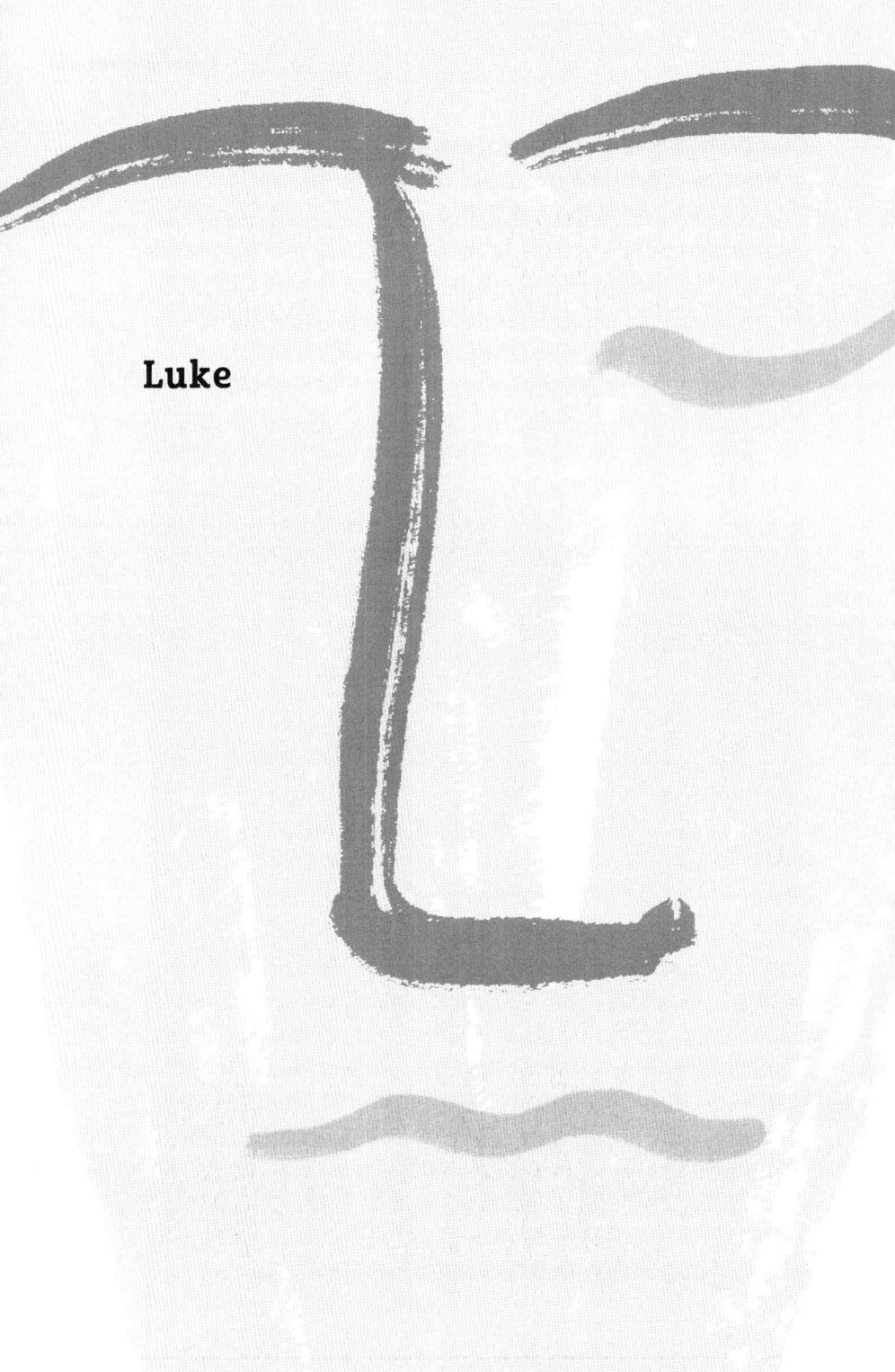

Luke

Luke

(Luke; Acts; Colossians 4:14;
2 Timothy 4:9-11; Philemon 23 - 24)

Most of us associate Luke with the third Gospel. However, he also wrote the Acts of the Apostles and may have played a role in composing other parts of the New Testament too, and accompanied Paul on some of his missionary journeys. Indeed, many will be surprised to discover that he wrote around a quarter of the New Testament, more than any other author, including Paul.

Neither the third Gospel nor the book of Acts mentions Luke by name, so why is it thought that someone called Luke wrote these books? Firstly, because church tradition holds Luke to be the author. For example, the earliest surviving manuscript of the third Gospel which dates from between AD 175 and 225 has the title "Gospel According to Luke" attached to it. Similarly, the Muratorian Canon, which is of a similar date and is an early list of New Testament books, also describes Luke as the author.[220] Early Church Fathers such as Irenaeus and Clement of Alexandria also believed he was the writer.

If someone called Luke wrote the third Gospel, he must also have written the book of Acts, because the two are so clearly connected. As well as the similarities in language, Acts clearly follows on from the Gospel. Both, for example, are addressed to someone called Theophilus and when addressing Theophilus in the book of Acts (1:1), the author refers to "the first book... I wrote about all that Jesus did and taught" (see also Luke 1:1-4). In addition, these two books seem to have a common aim running throughout them, to show the connection between Jesus' work and that of the Church, and to make clear that all that had happened to both was part of God's overarching plan. Acts, then, appears to be a sequel to the third Gospel. It is believed that the two books would originally have circulated together as a two-part work, but the Gospel was later separated from Acts and bound together with the other three Gospels.[221] This is why in our Bibles the book of Acts does not follow directly on from the Gospel of Luke as would be logical, but is separated from it by John's Gospel which, unfortunately, means the connection between the two is no longer obvious to readers.

Early church tradition refers to this Luke as a companion of Paul and this is supported by biblical evidence, too, of someone called Luke who worked closely with the apostle. In Paul's epistle to Philemon, which was probably written from his house arrest in Rome, Paul sent greetings from someone called Luke who he calls one of his "fellow-workers" (verse 24). In addition, the book of Acts seems to have been written by someone who travelled with Paul, for there are a number of what are known as "we" passages included in its descriptions of Paul's second and third missionary journeys. As the name implies, these passages were written in the first-person plural, suggesting the author was present. For instance, Acts 16:11 says "We set sail from Troas and took a straight course to Samothrace...", and Acts 28:16 declares, "When we came into Rome, Paul was allowed to live by himself...". Acts names a number of people who travelled with Paul, such as Aristarchus and Timothy, so none of these named companions is likely to be the author, for the writer would not refer to himself by the first person plural "we" in some parts of Acts and by his actual name in other verses. Of the remaining companions that Paul's letters show were with him in Rome (as the writer of the "we" passages appears to have been), Luke seems to be the most likely candidate.

These "we" sections were probably originally recorded in Luke's travel diary. They cover many exciting events in vivid detail, including Paul's shipwreck in Malta where he was bitten by a viper, the apostle's journey to Jerusalem where he met Jesus' brother James and the other leaders of that church, and his arrival in Rome where he was placed under house arrest. Indeed, it is claimed that Luke's description of his sea voyage to Rome with Paul is one of the most important documents on ancient seafaring in existence because of the detail it provides.[222]

Church and biblical tradition also hold that this Luke was not only a travelling companion but a doctor. Similarly, the letter to the Colossians, which many believe was written at a similar time to Philemon, when Paul was under house arrest in Rome, includes greetings from "Luke, the beloved physician" (4:14). Paul may have needed Luke to travel with him for his medical skills: his letters give us reason to suspect he was often not in great health. In his second letter to the Corinthian church (12:7-9) he talks of a "thorn in the flesh" that he prayed unsuccessfully for God to heal three times. This could have been an eye condition maybe connected with the blindness he suffered at the time of his conversion (Acts 9:8). In his letter to the Galatians (6:11) he says, "See what large letters I make when I am writing with my own hand!" suggesting he may have struggled with his sight. He also reminded the Galatians that "it was because of a physical infirmity that I first announced the Gospel to you" and described the extent of their concern for him back then by saying "you would have torn out your eyes and given them to me" suggesting, again, he had a problem affecting his sight (4:13-15). It is also possible that the physical ailments he suffered could have resulted from the beatings and other hardships he had endured on his missionary journeys.[223]

It has often been claimed that Luke's Gospel and Acts display more technical medical language than the other Gospels. However, many of the medical words Luke used were also employed by educated non-medics at the time and so, while their presence does not disprove he was a doctor, neither do they prove that he was.[224] Luke does, however, edit a story found in Mark's Gospel (5:26) in a way which may reflect his medical background. In the story of a woman who had been bleeding for twelve years, Mark candidly says: "She had endured much under many physicians, and had spent all she had; and she was no better, but grew rather worse." The version in Luke's Gospel (8:43) omits Mark's negative comments about the involvement of doctors, simply saying "though she had spent all she had on physicians, no one could cure her".

It is possible that Luke's first encounter with Paul came about because of his medical skills. The so-called "we" sections in Acts occur for the first time when Paul was at Troas, in modern-day Turkey, on his second missionary journey. He had not intended to visit this town; we are told that he and his travelling companions had wanted to go to Bithynia, but "the Spirit of Jesus did not allow them" (16:7-10). Luke, then, seems to have first met Paul in an encounter that had not been pre-arranged. This may suggest he was initially called upon for his medical services because Paul was again struggling with his health. Luke may then have gone on to encourage Paul to travel to Macedonia, in modern-day Greece, to preach the Gospel.[225] This was then confirmed by a vision Paul had of a man from that place pleading with him to

"Come over to Macedonia and help us" (verse 9). For us today this is a significant step, because by travelling to Macedonia Paul was for the first time preaching the Gospel in what is now Europe.

Why do some people think Luke may have encouraged Paul over to Macedonia? It has been suggested that Luke was from Macedonia himself, from the city of Philippi. There are several reasons for believing this. Firstly, he travelled with Paul as far as Philippi on his second missionary journey and then appears to have remained there rather than continuing to travel with Paul, for the first "we" passage does not continue beyond the description of their time in Philippi. The "we" sections do not resume again until Paul's next visit to Philippi which did not take place for another four to six years, suggesting Luke had spent the intervening time in that city. Luke also writes about Philippi in a way that implies great familiarity and fondness for the place. He described it as "a leading city of the district of Macedonia and a Roman colony" (Acts 16:12). This praise might indicate that he was proud of Philippi because it was his home town and it seems quite possible that Luke could have travelled between there and Troas as an itinerant doctor.[226]

Because it seems Luke remained in Philippi between his journeys with Paul, he may well have been in the city when Paul wrote his letter to the Philippians. If so, it is possible that he is actually referred to in that letter and may be the "loyal companion" Paul addresses towards the end of the epistle. This person was certainly someone Paul trusted, for he appealed to this companion to help a couple of female church members, Euodia and Syntyche, "to be of the same mind in the Lord", telling them to "help these women, for they have struggled beside me in the work of the Gospel" (4:2-3).

W e may assume Luke must have been well off to have
been a doctor. However, as we saw in our chapter on
Onesimus, many doctors were in fact slaves. Michael Card
puts forward an interesting theory that Luke may have been
one too. He says that many slaves were known by the
shortened form of their master's name and points out that
Paul had a relative who is mentioned in his letter to the Romans
(16:21) called Lucius. He speculates that, as Luke is a shortened
form of this name, Luke could have been the slave of Paul's
relative who freed him so he could work alongside Paul and
support him with his health.[227] This would explain why Luke
often records stories about people who were looked down
on in society – poor people, women and those who were
considered sinners, such as tax collectors. He may have been
able to afford to write his Gospel and Acts because he had
the patronage and support of someone of a higher rank, the
person he dedicates these works to, Theophilus. Theophilus
is mentioned at the start of both books. In his Gospel (1:3), Luke
writes that "I too decided... to write an orderly account for
you, most excellent Theophilus," and he starts Acts with "In the
first book, Theophilus, I wrote about all Jesus did and taught".

Theophilus appears to have been Luke's superior because
Luke addresses him as "most excellent", a term he uses
elsewhere of high-status people (Luke 1:3 compared with
Acts 23:6; 24:2-3; 26:25). This may explain why Luke took
pains in his writings to show that Christianity is not just for
those who are poor, but also those of higher rank, for he often
includes stories about such people acting positively towards
the Christian faith: for example Sergius Paulus, the pro-consul
of Paphos, Lydia, a dealer in expensive purple cloth, and the
centurion Cornelius (Acts 10; 13:7; 16:14-15). This may be
because he was trying to reassure Theophilus and other
high-status people that they had a place within Christianity.

We do not know who Theophilus was, but it seems he had heard about the Christian message and needed further instruction. At the beginning of his Gospel (1:4), Luke gives his reason for writing to Theophilus, saying it is "so that you may know the truth concerning the things about which you have been instructed". He says that to do this he is seeking to "set down an orderly account of the events that have been fulfilled among us, just as they were handed on to us by those who from the beginning were eyewitnesses and servants of the word". He says he is aiming to investigate "everything carefully from the very first" for Theophilus (verse 3). From this we learn several things. Firstly, Luke himself was not an eyewitness of everything he recorded. He did not know Jesus himself and was not present right from the start of the Church, although as we have seen he was involved in Paul's journeys and his later life. He did, though, seek out people who were eyewitnesses and talk to them. The first verse of his Gospel also suggests that when he wrote, there were other written accounts of Jesus' life in circulation, for he says, "many have undertaken to set down an orderly account of the events..."

It seems likely that Luke made use of some of these other accounts when writing his Gospel. One of these was Mark's Gospel. Just over half of Mark appears to have been included in Luke. However, Luke wrote much better Greek than Mark and often tidied up the parts he took from that Gospel. So, for example, he got rid of many of the connecting words Mark uses, such as "immediately", "and then" and "again".[228] He also made some of Mark's language more precise and accurate. For instance, Mark calls Herod Antipas a king when strictly speaking he was a tetrarch and Luke corrects that (Mark 6:14 and Luke 9:7). He also rephrases Mark's account of the parable of the sower, changing his explanation of why the seed failed to flourish on rocky ground from "it had no root" to the more accurate "it withered for lack of moisture".[229]

Luke did not just use Mark's work. Scholars believe he had access to a source which was also used by the writer of Matthew's Gospel. This is why Luke and Matthew contain some material that is not found in Mark. In addition, Luke also had his own sources and it seems he sought out eyewitnesses for himself who could give him information about Jesus and the life of the early Church, as the beginning of his Gospel suggests. Indeed, just over forty per cent of the material in Luke's Gospel is not found in any of the other three.[230] This includes much-loved parables such as the prodigal son and the good Samaritan. It also includes unique information about Jesus' and John the Baptist's births. If we did not have Luke's Gospel we would not have heard the story of the angels appearing to the shepherds to announce Jesus' birth, for instance, or Gabriel's visit to Mary to tell of her pregnancy.

It is possible that some of this unique material could have been gleaned during the time Luke is thought to have spent in Caesarea in Palestine. Acts (23:31 - 26:32) says Paul was imprisoned in that city for two years before he was transferred to Rome and put under house arrest. It seems likely that Luke stayed in Caesarea during Paul's imprisonment there, for we are told that he was with Paul in Jerusalem when the apostle was arrested (and it was from there that Paul was sent to Caesarea), and Luke was also present when the apostle was released from that prison two years later and sent to Rome for his trial (21:17 and 27:1 - 28:16). Caesarea was in Palestine, only about seventy miles from Jerusalem. It was also close to Galilee, so Luke could have used the two years Paul was imprisoned in that city, not only to support the apostle, but also to visit Christians in Palestine who had known Christ or had been involved in the beginnings of the early Church.

We also know from Acts that on his travels with Paul Luke spent time with several people who would have had information about the early Church. For instance, he visited Philip's house in Caesarea (21:8). Philip is described converting Samaritans and an Ethiopian eunuch and was a colleague of the first Christian martyr, Stephen (6:1-6; 8:4-40). Luke also stayed at the home of Mnason, who is referred to as "an early disciple", and he must have heard stories from him, too (21:16). Also, as mentioned in the chapter on Joanna, many believe Luke had a source at Herod Antipas' court, because he has material in his Gospel about Herod's role in Jesus' trial which is not found in the other Gospels – information he could have obtained from some of the characters he mentions in his writings who had connections to the Church and the court. These might have included Joanna's husband Chuza, who was Herod's steward, or Manaen, a member of the court of Herod (Luke 8:3; 23:6-12; Acts 13:1). And, of course, Luke was close to Paul and so must have got a lot of information about the early Church from him, too.

However, Luke was not just simply collecting information about the life of Jesus and the early Church and writing it all down; he had a theological purpose that helped him structure his work. He sought to show the spread of Christianity from Jerusalem to "all Judaea and Samaria, and to the ends of the earth" (Acts 1:8). As part of this, he made clear the link between Jesus' ministry and the early Church by showing that they were continuing Christ's work in their mission, healing in his name and empowered by his Spirit. This also involved showing how Christianity had developed from a Jewish religion to one that included many Gentiles, and making it clear that this was all part of God's long-term plan. It seems likely that one of Luke's aims in writing for Theophilus was to reassure him as a Gentile that non- Jews were welcome in the Church and considered a full part of God's people.

It is probable that Luke's own background may explain why he was so concerned to show that God's salvation plan included Gentiles as well as Jews. This is because, as many commentators believe, Luke himself was not Jewish. This idea is largely based on the passage in Colossians (4:10-14) in which Paul mentions those who were with him during his house arrest. He first mentions Mark, Aristarchus and Justus, who he says are "the only ones of the circumcision among my co-workers", meaning they were the only Jews with him. He then goes on to send greetings from Luke, suggesting that Luke was not one of Paul's circumcised companions and so was not Jewish. Indeed, Luke may well have been the only non-Jewish author in the whole of the New Testament. His interest in showing God's love for the Gentiles is not limited to his description of the Church's mission activity in Acts, but can be seen right from the start of his Gospel, where he traces Jesus' genealogy not just back to the father of the Jews, Abraham, as Matthew does, but to Adam, the father of all (Luke 3:23-38; Matthew 1:1-17). It is also reflected in his description of the angels' proclamation to the shepherds that Christ's birth is "good news of great joy for all the people" and Simeon's prophecy over the baby Jesus in the Temple that he would be "a light for revelation to the Gentiles" (Luke 2:10. 32).

We cannot overestimate the importance of Luke to our understanding of salvation. Not only does he show that God is the God of all, both those who are downtrodden and those who are influential, Gentile as well as Jew, but if it were not for his writings our understanding of the Christian message would be significantly depleted. We would know comparatively little about the early Church and Christians would have struggled to understand what their purpose was to be as they awaited Jesus' return. Indeed, the Christian faith would have been at risk of fizzling out when it became apparent that

Christ was not coming back anytime soon. But Luke teaches that there is a purpose to this intervening time; Christ's work has not stopped but continues through the mission of the Church until his return.

There is another reference to Luke in the New Testament, in 2 Timothy, that reveals a further remarkable thing about him: his faithfulness. This letter appears to have been written when Paul was in prison towards the end of his life, awaiting execution, for he talks of having "finished the race" and writes that the time of his departure has come (4:6-7). When this is understood in this context, the pathos of Paul's words really strike home. He writes to his fellow worker Timothy, "Do your best to come to me soon, for Demas, in love with this present world, has deserted me and gone to Thessalonica; Crescens has gone to Galatia, Titus to Dalmatia. Only Luke is with me" (verses 9-11a). It seems, then, that at the end of his life Paul was alone without his companions and in his hour of greatest need only Luke remained beside him. It is likely that this final imprisonment involved worse conditions than his earlier house arrest recorded in Acts. One place that has been suggested as the possible site of this imprisonment is the Mamertine dungeon in Rome. This can still be visited today and was a dark, cold underground cell that prisoners were lowered into by means of a hole in the roof.[23] If Paul was imprisoned in a place like this, then it is no wonder he felt so downcast, nor is it surprising that he asked Timothy to "bring the cloak that I left with Carpus at Troas" when he came to see him, for he would have been freezing in that cold, damp, underground hole (verse 13). It says a lot about Luke's character and his love for Paul that he would visit him in such desperate circumstances, and we can only wonder whether he remained with Paul right up until his execution by the sword.

Luke may have done even more than tend to Paul's health while he was imprisoned. It has been suggested that he acted as Paul's amanuensis (or secretary), helping him to write down his second letter to Timothy while he was in captivity, as well as the other so-called pastoral epistles, 1 Timothy and Titus, which were probably written from Philippi before his imprisonment. This is because the style of all three of these letters is very similar and they all contain many words not used in Paul's other letters, while sharing similarities with Luke's writings, both in terms of vocabulary and style.[232] This also fits with Luke being the only person who was with Paul when he was in prison and 2 Timothy was written.

It was not uncommon to use an amanuensis. Indeed, Paul's earlier use of one might be reflected in his letter to the Galatians (6:11), for as we have already seen he comments towards the end upon the large letters he made when writing in his "own hand", possibly suggesting the rest had been written by a scribe. An author would dictate their thoughts to an amanuensis who would write them down on wax tablets, probably in some form of shorthand, before writing them up onto papyrus.[233] As an amanuensis Luke may have been given the freedom to put Paul's thoughts into his own words, which would explain why the pastorals (1 and 2 Timothy and Titus) differ from Paul's other letters.

There is one big remaining mystery about Luke. Why did he finish the Acts of the Apostles where he did? The book ends without us being told what happened to Paul. We do not know whether he was released from house arrest in Rome or executed, something which is believed to have happened during the persecution of Christians ordered by the Emperor Nero. One answer is that Acts is not primarily about Paul, and Luke had achieved his goal by showing how Christianity reached Rome, which in his eyes proved the disciples had fulfilled Jesus' command to be his witnesses to "the ends of the earth" (Acts 1:8). However, another popular explanation is that Luke had planned a third volume to his story which would have included what happened to Paul after he was released from house arrest, but died before he could write it. One reason for believing this is that Acts is rougher in style than Luke's Gospel, suggesting he had had time to polish and revise his Gospel but may have died before he could do the same for Acts.[234] An ancient document, the Anti-Marcionite Prologue for Luke's Gospel, says that he died at the age of eighty-four in Boeotia, Greece.[235]

L uke appears to have been a modest and faithful man who was a tremendous support to Paul and who recorded momentous events in church history without feeling the need to draw undue attention to his own involvement in those events. We certainly owe Luke a great deal. His Gospel has left us much better informed about Jesus' life, providing us with a great deal of information, including treasured details about Jesus' birth, that is not found in the other Gospels. And in Acts Luke documents the years that followed Christ's death, including the growth of the early Church and its spread to the Gentiles. Without Luke we would know far less about early church history or the work of Paul and other early Christians who helped the Gospel move out from Jerusalem to the rest of the world.

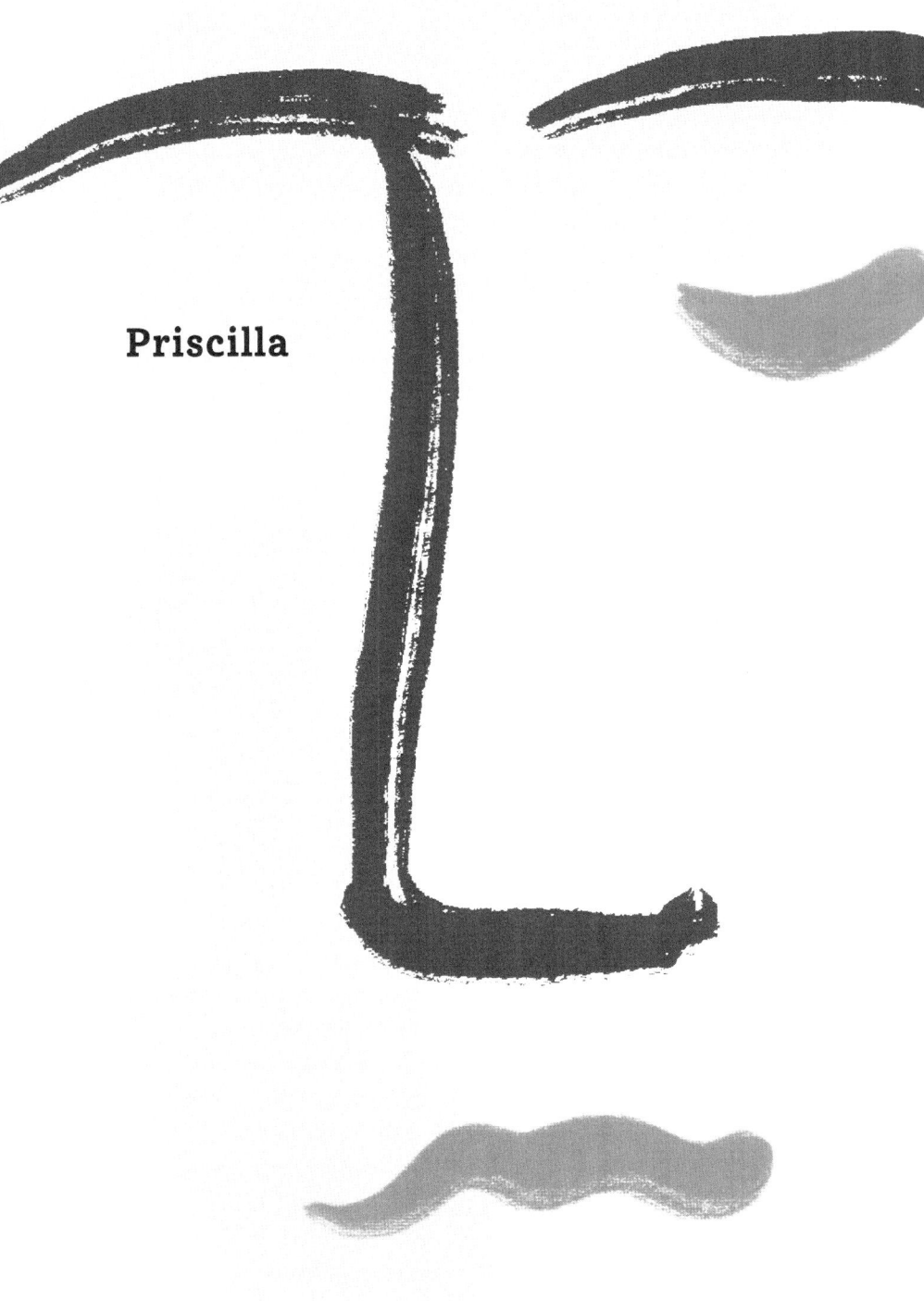

Priscilla

Priscilla

(Acts 18:1-4. 18. 24-28; Romans 16:3-4;
1 Corinthians 16:19; 2 Timothy 4:19)

Priscilla is mentioned in the Acts of the Apostles and several of Paul's letters. She was a close friend of Paul and played a key role in establishing churches in Rome, Corinth and Ephesus. She was also known by the more formal version of her name, Prisca, which is how Paul refers to her in his letters. Priscilla was married to a Jewish man called Aquila who came from the Roman province of Pontus on the Black Sea coast, in modern-day Turkey. The pair were a well-travelled, cosmopolitan couple, who spent time living in three different parts of the Roman Empire – Italy, Greece and Asia Minor. Priscilla's story offers us an insight into why Christianity was able to spread around the Roman Empire so easily; how the first churches began and the important role women played in them.

We first hear about Priscilla and Aquila when they are in the Greek city of Corinth. They had fled there because they and other Jews had been expelled from Rome by the Emperor Claudius (Acts 18:2). Most believe this is the same event that was described by the Roman historian Suetonius. He said this Jewish expulsion, of around AD 49, occurred because of disturbances that took place "at the instigation of Chrestus" and as Chrestus and the name Christos (or Christ) were pronounced the same way, the person Suetonius was talking about here is likely to have been Jesus and the disturbances he refers to were probably due to tensions that had arisen between Jews and Christians (including Jewish Christians like Aquila) when the Gospel was first preached in Rome.[236] Of course, Jesus was not around in AD 49 and never went to Rome, so could not have been involved in these disturbances, but Suetonius, writing seventy years later, probably did not realise this. He just assumed Christ must have been involved because he knew that Christians followed Jesus and wrongly believed him to be the ringleader of the riots.[237]

So it seems likely that Priscilla and Aquila were expelled from Rome because of their Christian activity. This suggests they were serious disciples who knew what it was like to be persecuted for their beliefs. And they appear to have been very early believers who found faith even before they'd met Paul, possibly through Roman Jews who had been in Jerusalem during Pentecost and had witnessed the outpouring of the Spirit. Many of these Jews became Christians and upon their return to Rome would have told others about their new-found faith (Acts 2:10).

It seems that despite a momentous move, of over seven hundred miles from Italy to Greece, Priscilla and Aquila were able to set up a home and business without difficulty in Corinth. They were tent-makers (or possibly leather-makers, as the Greek term could have this wider sense – tents in those days being made from leather).[238] It is possible that their tent-making business was so successful that they had branches in Rome, Corinth and Ephesus, which explains why they were able to settle so quickly in these places.[239]

It was because of their tent-making that they met Paul, who appears to have arrived in Corinth after Priscilla and Aquila. He was on his second missionary journey and had just visited

Athens. Corinth was an obvious place to travel to next as it was a very important city, the capital of its province.

When Paul stayed a good length of time in one place, as he did in Corinth, he often worked to fund his travels by finding employment as a tent-maker, the same trade as Priscilla and Aquila (Acts 18:2-3. 11). Therefore, his missionary journeys were not taken up with preaching alone. When he was tent-making, he probably only had time to preach on the sabbath and was caught up with manual work the rest of the week.[240] Indeed, there is evidence that he laboured even longer hours than most, for in his first letter to the Thessalonians (2:9) he talks about working night and day so as not to be a burden to the Church. This suggests that Paul was not a wealthy man who was able to fund his travels without working and that he struggled financially at times. In his first letter to the Corinthians (4:11), for instance, he talks of being hungry, thirsty and "poorly clothed".

There are several possible reasons why Paul chose to work while he was on his missionary travels rather than simply rely on financial support from fellow Christians. He would not have wanted to burden his new converts or lay himself open to the accusation that he was preaching for financial gain, as other travelling teachers were, and he may also have been concerned that receiving money from others would lead them to demand something in return, as favours were expected to be repaid in Roman society. Some congregations could, for instance, have used the fact they had given Paul financial support to pressurise him to remain at their churches longer, which would have made it difficult to move on and continue his mission.

Being employed in manual labour would have affected Paul's status in the eyes of some, for such occupations were often looked down upon by the well-to-do of the Roman world.[242]

Paul seems to have viewed this as a necessary sacrifice, for he counted being "weary from the work" of his hands as one of the costs of being an apostle (1 Corinthians 4:12).

So when Paul arrived in Corinth one of the first things he would have done was seek out a fellow tent-maker who was able to offer him some work. Other tent-makers would not have been difficult to find, for people of similar trades often had businesses close to each other and there would have been a Jewish quarter, where he could find people of a similar background.[243] Meeting a couple like Priscilla and Aquila could not have come at a better time for Paul, for, as he told the Corinthian church in his first letter to them (2:3), he came to their city "in weakness and in fear and in much trembling". We do not know why he felt so down. Perhaps it was the tough time he had just had in Athens where some had "scoffed" when he preached about the resurrection of the dead (Acts 17:32). He may also have been missing the company of Timothy and Silas, who had stayed behind in Macedonia when he'd been forced to flee due to hostile crowds. He was not fully reunited with them until later on in his time in Corinth (verses 13-15; 18:5). At this low point in his ministry Priscilla and Aquila's friendship would have been particularly important.

Acts (18:4) tells us that while in Corinth, Paul spent every sabbath arguing in the synagogue, trying to persuade people about Christ. It seems likely that Priscilla and Aquila helped him in this work, and so would have been crucial in founding the Corinthian church. Paul must have been encouraged by the response to the Gospel in Corinth for, despite significant opposition, his ministry bore much fruit: the synagogue official, Crispus, and his entire household came to faith as well as many other Corinthians (verses 5-8).

Paul also received a vision from God (verses 9-11), instructing him to remain in the city, which he did for eighteen months. This reminds us that his missionary journeys involved more than moving from place to place preaching; he also stayed in some cities for a considerable amount of time in order to establish worshipping communities.

After Corinth, Paul travelled to Ephesus, taking Priscilla and Aquila with him (Acts 18:18-19). This was another significant journey which involved sailing across the Aegean Sea into what was yet another region of the Roman Empire, Asia Minor. So, having already sailed from Rome in Italy all the way to Corinth in Greece, Priscilla and Aquila were now heading to Ephesus, in modern-day Turkey, a journey of nearly five hundred miles. In those days there were no passenger ships. They would have had to travel to the port to try and find a cargo boat that was heading their way, taking with them basics like food, pots, pans and bedding for the journey, and once aboard they would have had to sleep in the open air or in little tents erected on the decks.[244]

Travelling by sea was dependent on wind power. This meant that even after they had found a vessel, they may well have had to wait around at the port for the wind direction and strength to be favourable and for good sea conditions. Even then the wind could still turn against them en route, making their journey time much longer.

How was it possible for Priscilla and Aquila to settle so easily in cities that today are within completely different countries? The reason was that despite the great distances between them, they were all part of the Roman Empire. As this vast empire stretched from Spain in the West to Syria in the East, the same coins were accepted throughout, so Priscilla would not have had to exchange her money for other currencies on any of her journeys and there were no language barriers within the Roman Empire, for most people could speak either Greek (the language in which the New Testament is written) or Latin.[245] Therefore, although Priscilla and Aquila travelled to and lived in many different places, all these cities had a huge amount in common.

Travellers like Priscilla and Aquila also benefited from the legacy of the former emperor Augustus. He had carried out a programme of road restoration and bridge-building. This meant there were excellent routes to all the major cities of the empire and Augustus also made travelling safer by policing these routes, so people were protected from robbery on the roads as well as piracy at sea.

E phesus was another important city which, like Corinth, was strategic for travel as it was near the coast and a gateway into Asia. It was most famous for the temple of the goddess Artemis which was considered one of the seven wonders of the ancient world. The worship of Artemis would, however, cause Paul significant problems, as we shall see later. But on this occasion he did not stay long in the city, just managing to squeeze in a visit to the local synagogue where he again disputed with people about Jesus (Acts 18:19-21). Paul was keen to travel on to Jerusalem because he had made a vow, probably a Nazirite vow, which involved not cutting his hair for a period of time (verse 18). This was a way of offering thanks to God and Paul had a lot to thank God for, such as his friendship with Priscilla and Aquila and the success of the mission in Corinth. Paul's vow ended with shaving off his hair, which he did before sailing for Ephesus. He wanted to present this hair as a burnt offering in the Temple at Jerusalem. He was keen to continue his journey in order to do that, but he left Priscilla and Aquila behind in Ephesus to continue with their tent-making, and perhaps with the hope that they would carry on with missionary activities while he was gone.[246]

While Priscilla and Aquila were without Paul in Ephesus they had a very fortuitous encounter. They met a man from Alexandria in Egypt called Apollos (Acts 18:24-28). We are told that Apollos was "an eloquent man, well-versed in the scriptures" which is unsurprising because Alexandra was the centre of Jewish learning. It appears Apollos had learnt something of the Christian faith and "spoke with burning enthusiasm and taught accurately the things concerning Jesus". However, on hearing him preach, Priscilla and Aquila had some concerns. For all his fervour and enthusiasm, Apollos only knew about the baptism offered by John the Baptist, which presumably meant he had not been taught about Christian baptism. Priscilla and Aquila took Apollos under their wing and "explained the way of God to him more accurately". They were clearly happy that Apollos had benefited from their instruction, because we are told that the Ephesian Christians, who presumably included Priscilla and Aquila, supported Apollos in his desire to go and do God's work in Achaia, where the Corinthian church was, and they sent letters recommending Apollos to the believers there.

Luke leaves us in no doubt that Priscilla and Aquila's teaching bore great fruit. He informs us that on his arrival in Achaia, Apollos "greatly helped those who through grace had become believers, for he powerfully refuted the Jews in public, showing by the scriptures that the Messiah is Jesus" (Acts 18:27-28). This is backed up by what we discover about Apollos in Paul's letters to the Corinthian church. It appears that he was very popular with many believers there. Indeed, he seems to have had something of a fan club because some in the church were claiming they belonged to Apollos rather than Paul, meaning they favoured Apollos possibly because his preaching was more impressive than the apostle's (1 Corinthians 1:10-13). Paul, himself, conceded that he did not use "lofty words", but kept his preaching simple and focused upon Christ's crucifixion.

He was conscious of criticisms circulating among the Corinthians that he did not come across as powerfully in his public speaking as he did in his letters (2:1-5; 2 Corinthians 10:10). It seems likely, then, that Paul's preaching contrasted markedly with the fine words and fervour of Apollos. Paul, though, did not accept this factionalism but addressed it head on, reminding the Corinthians that he and Apollos had different gifts and roles but worked together for the good of the Church (1 Corinthians 3:5-9). There is no evidence that Apollos himself did anything to encourage this rivalry. Indeed, it appears he was deeply embarrassed by it, for he later refused to return to Corinth even though Paul strongly urged him to, probably because he was concerned that his presence would stir up more trouble for Paul (16:12).

The training of Apollos tells us a lot about Priscilla. She was no junior partner in this endeavour. When Luke describes the couple teaching Apollos, it is Priscilla's name that is mentioned first before her husband's. Because this was unusual at the time, it implies she played an important role in teaching him rather than simply acting as her husband's assistant. Indeed, of the six occasions this couple are mentioned in the New Testament, Priscilla is named first four times (Acts 18:18. 26; Romans 16:3; 2 Timothy 4:19). Indeed, many think she was mentioned first because she was more prominent in the church than her husband. Not only did Priscilla teach a man, but she gave instruction to a man who was very well educated and who, we are also told, was "well-versed in the scriptures". She must, then, have been a very competent, educated woman herself, as Luke makes it clear that her instruction of Apollos was very successful.

Priscilla's teaching role in Ephesus, though, does appear to be at odds with later instructions given in 1 Timothy (2:12) about the Ephesian church, which the RSV Bible translates as, "I permit no woman to teach or to have authority over a man; she is to keep silent".

How can this apparent dichotomy be explained? Was Priscilla only allowed to teach a man because she was doing it in partnership with her husband or because she was teaching Apollos in a private capacity rather than in a church service? These explanations seem unlikely. As we have seen, Luke appears to present Priscilla as the driving force in the teaching of Apollos. It also seems unlikely that a woman would be forbidden to teach a man in church services (which took place in people's homes – often women's) but would be allowed to instruct a man when fewer people were present. It also seems unlikely that women would be barred from positions of authority when there is evidence of them playing just such roles elsewhere in the New Testament: Phoebe, for instance, was a "deacon" and "benefactor" at the church of Cenchreae (Romans 16:1-3). Also, as we have seen in our chapter on Joanna, there was probably a female apostle called Junia, and women clearly prophesied – a gift Paul considered particularly important (Acts 21:9; Romans 16:7; 1 Corinthians 11:5; 14:1).

M any, therefore, have suggested that these instructions given to Timothy (1 Timothy 2:12) were a response to a specific situation that had arisen in the Ephesian church. This difficult verse can be translated in a number of ways and the Greek verb often rendered as "authority" may actually carry a more negative sense: it may suggest an overbearing attitude. Therefore, rather than banning women from teaching *and* having authority over men, this verse is more likely to condemn the overbearing way in which the women were teaching the men. This appears to be the sense in which the International Standard Version of the Bible has understood the verse, for it has translated it as: "Moreover, in the area of teaching, I am not allowing a woman to instigate conflict against a man".

Ben Witherington is someone who, among others, holds this view. He argues that this domineering attitude may have arisen among well-to-do females in the congregation. They thought their high status gave them the right to teach men in an overly authoritative manner, even though they had not yet received adequate training in the Christian message themselves. This is likely to have been especially concerning because some, at least, of these women may have come under the influence of false teachers. Witherington argues that the ban on women teaching men in Ephesus did not arise because Paul had an objection in principle to women teaching. Instead, he shows how the Greek of this verse means that Paul did not permit women to teach at that particular moment, rather than declaring a for-all-time ban, implying this prohibition could be overturned if women were trained well in the future. Priscilla, in contrast to these other women, was able to instruct Apollos admirably, and presumably with Paul's approval, because she was well educated and had been well instructed by the apostle himself.

The women's attitudes may have been influenced by the heresies rife in the Ephesian church. This heretical teaching may have involved a rejection of marriage and childbearing and could have stemmed from a warped view of the Adam and Eve story which held the male sex to be responsible for sin because of Adam and emboldened women to try and dominate men.[248] The centrality of the temple of Artemis may have encouraged such heresies. Women played a major role in the worship of this goddess and all the priests serving in the temple of Artemis were women. It is possible that this passage reflects an attempt to encourage female learning (which was unusual at the time) while making it clear to the Ephesians that this did not mean the Church should operate like the Artemis cult where women dominated men.[249]

So, whatever the exact nature of the problem at Ephesus was, it seems there is good reason to believe it had something to do with overbearing teaching. This was not a failing of which Priscilla had been guilty, however – her teaching was only ever extolled. And she appears to have continued to be held in high esteem by Paul and the Ephesian churches in the years after these difficult verses in 1 Timothy were written, for in a later letter to Timothy Paul tells him to "Greet Prisca and Aquila", suggesting the pair continued to play a significant role in the church after these problems had broken out (2 Timothy 4:19).

Priscilla's influential role in church life was not limited to teaching; she also hosted churches in many of the homes in which she lived. When writing to the Corinthians from Ephesus, for instance, Paul says, "The churches of Asia send greetings. Aquila and Prisca, together with the church in their house, greet you warmly in the Lord" (1 Corinthians 16:19). Priscilla, then, clearly played a vital role in the Christian community of Ephesus and when the couple returned to Rome, they established a house church in that city too, for Paul sent his greetings to "the church in their house" when he wrote to the Romans (16:3-5).

These house churches were far more than modern-day house groups (midweek meetings in people's homes held in addition to Sunday services). House churches such as Priscilla's were the only form of church in those days, because for the first few centuries Christians did not have places of worship. As many believers were either slaves with no homes of their own or poor people living in cramped conditions, the only way early Christians would have been able to meet in sizable groups was if the richer believers, people like Priscilla and Aquila, were prepared to use their larger homes in God's service, opening them up for

congregations to gather and worship.[250] There may have been
a number of these small house churches in a city, each hosting
possibly around thirty people, perhaps even as many as sixty
if some also stood in the courtyards of these larger homes.[251]
A number of house churches are mentioned in the New
Testament in addition to the ones hosted by Priscilla and
Aquila. Philemon had one in his home in Colossae; Lydia
"a dealer in purple cloth" hosted a church at Philippi and
another took place in the house of someone called Nympha
(Acts 16:40; Colossians 4:15; Philemon 1*b*-2).

We have seen that there was a close friendship between
Paul and Priscilla and her husband: they were his support
and encouragement during his time in Corinth and he felt
confident enough in their ability to leave them at Ephesus to
prepare the ground for his later missionary work there. And it
seems that Paul's faith in this couple was well founded. In his
letter to the Romans he not only described them as working
with him in Christ but says that they "risked their necks for
my life" (Romans 16:4).

Unfortunately, we do not know in what way they risked
their lives for Paul. It seems most likely that this happened
during their time in Ephesus. Acts (19:23-41) records one
violent incident that occurred after Paul had returned to the
city which may be connected with their heroic act. Demetrius,
a silversmith who made silver shrines, stirred up trouble towards
the apostle – these were probably small models of the temple
of Artemis.[252] As we have seen, this temple was central to
Ephesian life and many made a good living from producing
these replicas. But because Paul had been challenging their
idolatry and had consequently threatened their livelihood,
Demetrius inflamed the crowd against him.

Two of Paul's fellow workers were seized by an angry mob and dragged to the city's open-air theatre. We are told that Paul "wished to go into the crowd", perhaps to explain his point of view or to intervene on his friends' behalf, but the disciples would not let him. Could Priscilla and Aquila have been among those who prevented Paul from entering the baying mob and was it in these violent circumstances that they risked their lives to defend the apostle? We do not know. Paul may well have been referring to another incident. After all, he was no stranger to persecution, for in his writings he mentions being beaten a number of times in the course of his missionary work as well as being stoned (2 Corinthians 11:25). In his letters to the Corinthians he also describes trouble at Ephesus, which could be connected with the problems caused by Demetrius and his rioting mob, or might refer to other dangers that we are not told about. He writes to the Corinthians (1 Corinthians 15:32) that "I fought with wild animals at Ephesus", which is probably a metaphorical reference to some sort of opposition. He also describes "the affliction" he experienced in Asia and how it has left him and others "so utterly, unbearably crushed that we despaired of life itself" (2 Corinthians 1:8). Paul has clearly been through some very dangerous situations and it appears that Priscilla and her husband were right alongside him, in at least some of these.

It seems that sometime after this, Priscilla and Aquila returned to Rome. This may have simply been because the Emperor Claudius, who had expelled them, had now died, or perhaps their departure from Ephesus was a consequence of the antagonism Paul experienced there. But even then, it seems their travels did not stop, for as we have already seen, Priscilla and Aquila are mentioned again in 2 Timothy, which suggests they had returned to Ephesus. This couple, then, served the Lord wherever they went, using their assets to further God's purposes by hosting churches in their homes. Priscilla was a gifted teacher who helped with Paul's missionary endeavours in Corinth and Ephesus, supported and encouraged the apostle in difficult times and even risked her life for him. Not only did Priscilla play a vital role in God's mission, but her friendship with Paul reflects well on the character of the apostle himself.

Many have accused Paul of being a misogynist, due to some of the difficult passages about women in his letters. Yet it has been pointed out that an educated, intelligent woman like Priscilla is hardly likely to have risked her life for Paul if he was the unpleasant male chauvinist he is often portrayed to be.[253]

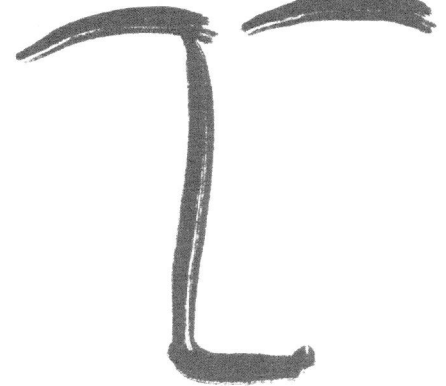

Timothy

Timothy

(Acts 16:1-5; 17:14-15; 18:5; 19:22; 20:2-5;
Romans 16:21; 1 Corinthians 4:17; 16:10-11;
2 Corinthians 1:1. 19; Philemon 1:1*a*; 2:19-24;
Colossians 1:1; 1 Thessalonians 1:1; 3:1-6;
2 Thessalonians 1:1; 1 Timothy; 2 Timothy;
Hebrews 13:23)

Timothy was a co-worker of Paul and was probably the colleague to whom Paul felt closest. He is mentioned in all but three of the New Testament letters associated with Paul. He even has two New Testament epistles addressed to him, 1 and 2 Timothy. As Timothy is the most frequently mentioned of Paul's colleagues, we learn a lot about him – his frailties and shortcomings as well as his tremendous strengths. Timothy's story encourages us all that we do not have to be perfect to do God's work.

It seems likely that Paul originally came across this young man on his first missionary journey with Barnabas when he visited Timothy's home village of Lystra (Acts 14:6-23; 16:1). Lystra was in Galatia, which is in modern-day Turkey. Paul's first visit there had been eventful: his healing of a man had led the pagan locals to declare him to be the god Hermes. But this adoration quickly changed when some antagonistic Jews from nearby towns whipped up the crowd against the apostle which led to Paul being stoned (Acts 14:8-20). Despite the troubles Paul faced in Lystra, it seems Timothy, his mother Eunice and his grandmother Lois all became Christians as

a result of his missionary activities there (2 Timothy 1:5).
Indeed, in his letters Paul often referred to Timothy as his
"child", which suggests he was his convert (1 Corinthians 4:17;
1 Timothy 1:2. 18; 2 Timothy 2:1).

B y the time Paul met Timothy again, on his second
missionary journey, the young man had grown in his faith
to such an extent that we are told "he was well spoken of
by the believers in Lystra and Iconium" (Acts 16:2). Iconium
was about twenty miles from Lystra. For Timothy's reputation
to be known that far outside his own village suggests this
young man had made quite an impression and may have
spent time working with believers in neighbouring towns.
All this was not lost on Paul. Two important members of
his team – Barnabas and John Mark – had recently left Paul
after a disagreement. Paul had recruited Silas as a replacement
for Barnabas and he may well have seen Timothy as someone
who could take on John Mark's old assistant role. John Mark
had pulled out of Paul's earlier missionary journey before it
was complete, so this time Paul would have been looking
for a young person who was more resilient and better able
to cope with the challenge.

To leave his village, mother and grandmother to travel so far
from home must have been a massive decision for Timothy.
He was probably only between eighteen and twenty-one
at the time.[254] Despite his young age, he would have been acutely
aware of the dangers involved in missionary work.
After all, Paul had been stoned and left for dead in Timothy's
own village. But Paul never attempted to hide the cost of
discipleship. For instance, we are told that he taught his new
disciples, "it is through many persecutions that we must
enter the kingdom of God" (Acts 14:22*b*).

Timothy's upbringing had given him a solid foundation in the scriptures, which must have been a help in his new role. At this very early stage of Christianity there was no New Testament, so for these Christians their scriptures were the books that make up our Old Testament and it seems Timothy's Jewish mother had brought him up to know these well. Paul wrote to Timothy saying, "from childhood you have known the sacred writings that are able to instruct you for salvation through faith in Christ Jesus" (2 Timothy 3:15). It was customary for Jewish children to be taught the scriptures from five years of age, so Timothy would have been learning about them for a long time and would have had a good grounding in them.

There were other things about Timothy's background that presented Paul with real difficulties. When he arrived at a new place, Paul often began his preaching at the local synagogue. Bringing Timothy along to these synagogues would have caused offence, for although Timothy had a Jewish mother, he had not been circumcised. This was probably because his father was not Jewish and may not have been keen on the practice. However, in the eyes of the Jews as the son of a Jewish mother it seems likely that Timothy would be seen as Jewish himself and would have been expected to be circumcised. Paul was already facing opposition from some Jews, as his stoning in Lystra illustrates, and he was particularly concerned not to antagonise them further. One of the grievances some Jews had against Paul was their belief that he was encouraging Jewish Christian converts to abandon their heritage and religious practices. Having a companion who was an uncircumcised Jew would only have fuelled such beliefs.

We are told that Paul had Timothy circumcised "because of the Jews who were in those places" (Acts 16:3*b*). It surprises many, though, that Paul would do such a thing because his letters show him strongly opposing false teachers who had been going around his churches telling his Gentile believers they had to be circumcised to be saved. However, Timothy's situation was different from Paul's Gentile converts, for although he had a Greek father he was not considered a Gentile because of his Jewish mother. Therefore, Paul would not have thought it a problem to circumcise Timothy, for the young man already had a Jewish background. Also, Paul took this action to overcome a barrier to his missionary work among the Jews rather than because he believed circumcision was necessary for Timothy's salvation. Even so, the decision is likely to have been misunderstood and may have fuelled claims that some of the false teachers in places like Galatia appear to have been making – that Paul, like them, thought Gentile believers should be circumcised (Galatians 5:11). Paul must have really believed there was something special about Timothy to bring him along on his missionary journeys when whatever choice he made, whether he circumcised the young man or not, would have drawn criticism and misunderstanding from one group or another. Timothy, too, must have been very committed to travelling with Paul when this meant not only leaving the security of home at a young age but undergoing a painful intimate procedure.

There was another reason why Timothy may have been a controversial choice to join a mission that involved reaching out to Jews as well as Gentiles – Timothy's mixed heritage. Marriage between Jews and Gentiles was frowned upon by many Jews and some may even have considered children of such marriages, like Timothy, illegitimate.[255] All this, again, suggests that Paul was so impressed with this young man that people's negative attitudes towards him did not discourage the apostle from recruiting him.

Perhaps part of the reason for Paul's attachment to Timothy was that he had paternal feelings towards this young man. Most think Timothy's father was no longer alive and it is likely that

Paul was either widowed or had never been married because he encourages the Christians in Corinth "to remain unmarried as I am" (1 Corinthians 7:8), and so he may not have had children of his own. The age gap between the two men may have encouraged Paul to see Timothy paternally. Certainly, the apostle would later write to the Philippians (2:22) about Timothy saying how he had served him "in the work of the Gospel... like a son with a father".

Despite Paul's attachment to the young man, Timothy did not receive a gentle introduction to missionary work. Firstly, he had to get used to their travel plans frequently changing which must have been very unsettling. Acts (16:6-7) tells us, somewhat mysteriously, that Paul's missionary team was "forbidden by the Holy Spirit" from speaking the word in Asia and that "they attempted to go into Bithynia, but the Spirit of Jesus did not allow them". They ended up sailing over to Macedonia as a result of a vision Paul had and also visiting Philippi (verses 9-10). As well as not having the security of knowing in advance exactly where they would be going, there was also much danger. In Philippi Paul and Silas got into an altercation with a slave owner after they had cast "a spirit of divination" out of his slave girl, preventing her from making money through fortune telling. Paul and Silas were dragged into the marketplace, stripped and "beaten with rods", receiving a "severe flogging" before being thrown in prison (verses 16-40). It is hard to believe Timothy did not suffer at the hands of the violent mob too; Luke often only mentions what happened to the main characters in events, so it is possible that Timothy may have been thrown into prison as well. Even if he was fortunate enough to escape the violence, witnessing such traumatic events, especially at his young age, must have shaken him. We can only imagine how distressed he was watching his mentors, Paul and Silas, beaten and hauled off to a prison cell. It must also have been very frightening to be alone in a strange and hostile town knowing he, too, could end up beaten and arrested.

Even after Paul and Silas were out of their prison cell, the
danger continued. When they reached Thessalonica, a mob of
disgruntled Jews and local "ruffians" stirred up trouble in the
town, trying to find Paul and Silas. How frightening it must have
been hiding from a violent mob. They fled to Beroea, but the
same frenzied rabble followed them there and incited the crowd
there too. Things got so dangerous that Paul had to flee and head
for Athens, leaving Silas and Timothy in Beroea (Acts 17:1-15).

What an introduction to the missionary life for Timothy!
He witnessed the highs of miracles and conversions
which must have sent his faith soaring, but also experienced
persecution and may have even suffered violence. He must
have quickly learnt the truth of Paul's teaching that suffering
goes hand in hand with serving Christ. Paul would later remind
Timothy of everything he had seen him suffer on this missionary
journey in order to encourage him:

> *now you have observed my teaching, my conduct, my aim in life,
> my faith, my patience, my love, my steadfastness, my persecutions,
> and my suffering the things that happened to me in Antioch,
> Iconium, and Lystra. What persecutions I endured! Yet the
> Lord rescued me from them all. (2 Timothy 3:10-11)*

It seems that Paul viewed Timothy as his apprentice, who
would learn by working alongside him, witnessing him in
action and seeing how he dealt with problems.

Having to abruptly flee Beroea and leave Timothy and his
other friends behind was something that Paul seems to have
found as upsetting as Timothy did. The apostle did not like being
alone, especially not in Athens, where there were no believers
to support him and he was surrounded by images of pagan
gods. He made sure that those who had helped him escape to
Athens returned to Beroea with instructions for Silas and Timothy

"to join him as soon as possible" (Acts 17:15-16). We often think of Paul as an independent, fearless pioneer but he was, in fact, very much a team player who loved to work alongside others.

Paul's first letter to the Thessalonians suggests that Timothy did reunite with Paul in Athens. However, the apostle was so anxious about the new converts he had been forced to leave behind in Thessalonica and the hostile environment they faced, that he sent Timothy back to Thessalonica to find out how they were getting on and to encourage them, even though that meant he was all alone in Athens again. He wrote to the Thessalonian believers:

> *when we could bear it no longer, we decided to be left alone in Athens; and we sent Timothy, our brother and co-worker for God in proclaiming the Gospel of Christ, to strengthen and encourage you for the sake of your faith, so that no one would be shaken by these persecutions. (1 Thessalonians 3:1-3a)*

This marks the start of a new role for Timothy as Paul's envoy, travelling to places Paul was not able to go, either because he was a wanted man, as in Thessalonica, or because he did not have time to revisit churches due to other missionary commitments. This suggests that Paul felt Timothy had matured enough to manage such a task and shows the young man had bravery, for he was prepared to return to Thessalonica, a city where they had dangerous and violent enemies. This new role would have been very important in an age where any letters had to be carried by associates of Paul across sea and land. As Paul founded more and more congregations around the Roman Empire, it became increasingly difficult for him to keep tabs on them all. This caused the apostle a great deal of anxiety, especially when these Christians had not been believers for long and often faced hostility. He longed to find out how they were coping and whether they were continuing in their faith.

so Timothy's role in providing this information was invaluable. Indeed, in one of his letters Paul talks of being "under daily pressure because of my anxiety for all the churches" (2 Corinthians 11:28).

Timothy was reunited with Paul in Corinth, where the apostle had moved after Athens, and brought good news about the Thessalonian church. Paul mentions what Timothy reported in his first letter to the Thessalonians (3:6):

> *Timothy has just now come to us from you, and has brought us the good news of your faith and love. He has told us also that you always remember us kindly and long to see us - just as we long to see you.*

It seems likely that Timothy also told Paul some of the problems the Thessalonians were facing and some of the questions they had about their faith, which Paul went on to address in his letter (4:3-8. 13 - 5:11). These included problems with sexual immorality as well as questions about Jesus' return and whether those who died before he came back would miss out on being with Christ.

Luke does not make it clear how long Timothy spent in Corinth with Paul or whether he continued travelling with him after the apostle left for Ephesus with Aquila and Priscilla. However, it seems that Timothy was in Ephesus when Paul returned to the city as part of his third missionary journey. This time the apostle stayed there for around three years and Timothy appears to have been with him for at least some of that time.[256] Again, he continued to act as Paul's envoy and one of the situations into which he was sent proved particularly difficult – his trip to Corinth.

Paul had sent a letter that we no longer possess to the Corinthian church warning them to avoid immoral behaviour. Later he received news that things had continued to deteriorate there, and the church was splitting into factions. So he wrote the letter we know as 1 Corinthians to address these problems, and also sent Timothy to this city. However, Paul clearly had some concerns about how Timothy would be received by the Corinthians, for he warned them to ensure that his young co-worker had "nothing to fear among you, for he is doing the work of the Lord just as I am; therefore let no one despise him. Send him on his way in peace" (1 Corinthians 16:10-11a).

Timothy was no stranger to the Corinthian church. He had spent time there with Paul as we have already seen. So at first sight it is surprising that Paul would warn them not to despise Timothy when they had witnessed him working alongside the apostle. What lay behind Paul's concerns? Firstly, Timothy was going to Corinth as Paul's representative. Paul said he was sending him to remind the Corinthians "of my ways in Christ Jesus, as I teach them everywhere in every church" (1 Corinthians 4:17). This was not going to be an easy task because there was a lot of criticism of Paul in Corinth. People were saying things like: "I belong to Paul", "I belong to Apollos", or "I belong to Cephas [Peter]", which implies they were setting different Christian leaders against each other and picking their favourite (1:12). If Paul was facing criticism at Corinth and Timothy was going there to represent Paul, it is no wonder the apostle was worried about how the young man would be received.

However, this was not the only problem Timothy faced. It seems there was some resentment that Paul was not coming to see them himself. In his first letter Paul mentions some who thought he was not going to visit them again and had become arrogant as a result (1 Corinthians 4:18). There may have been rumours circulating that he did not have the courage to come and address his criticism of them face to face.[257] These grumbles are likely to have been compounded by Paul sending Timothy, a far less senior figure, instead. After all, the Corinthians saw Timothy as Paul's assistant and someone who was younger than the other co-workers familiar to them such as Silas, Aquila and Priscilla. Hence, Paul stressed Timothy's credentials, making it clear that he had sent him because he was the best person for the job, for he was his "beloved and faithful child in the Lord", someone as close to himself as it was possible to be (verse 17).

It also seems likely that Timothy's age was a factor in their attitude towards him. In later years when Timothy had been deployed by Paul to deal with problems in the church at Ephesus, Paul wrote to him saying, "let no one despise your youth" (1 Timothy 4:12*a*). Timothy was a mature man by this stage and so it might seem strange that he was still being called a youth. However, people were often not given official positions until they reached the age of fifty and were referred to as young up until their forties.[258] Timothy's authority appears to have been challenged in Ephesus because he was younger than those he was having to reprimand, even though he was no longer by our standards a youth. It is often suggested that this may have been more of an issue because Timothy appears not to have been a confident person. If his young age and lack of confidence were an issue in Ephesus, it is even more likely to have been a problem in Corinth, for he was probably in his twenties then and would have been even younger and less experienced.

Indeed, Paul's fears about how the Corinthians would treat Timothy proved to be well founded. Timothy's mission was not a success. The Corinthians did not respond well to Paul's letter or listen to Timothy, so Paul was forced to interrupt his work in Ephesus in order to visit the church himself and try and sort the problems out. However, his visit did not go well either, Paul himself calling it "painful" (2 Corinthians 2:1).

Things did not improve until Paul sent the believers a particularly severe letter delivered by another of his co-workers, Titus, who seems to have been able to get the church into line. Indeed, Paul records that the church welcomed Titus "with fear and trembling" (7:13-15). This leaves us with some intriguing questions. How would Timothy have felt to be replaced as the envoy to Corinth by someone else and see that person succeed where he had failed? How badly was his confidence knocked by all the confrontation and opposition he had experienced? He was used to persecution from people who were not Christians, but it must have come as a shock to be treated so badly by his brothers and sisters in Christ. The whole experience is likely to have left him shaken.

H owever, we should remember that Timothy was not the only one to struggle with the situation at Corinth. Paul had found it difficult to win over the Corinthians, too. Indeed, it has been argued that Paul's keenness to push his protégé forward may have been an error of judgement on his part, for it forced Timothy into a difficult situation he was not yet ready to deal with.[259] Paul, though, knew that God does not always pick leaders who align with the world's ideas of leadership. As he wrote to the Corinthians, "God chose what is weak in the world to shame the strong; God chose what is low and despised in the world" (1 Corinthians 1:27-28a). This belief may well have been one reason why he did not let Timothy's youth or lack of confidence prevent him from sending him out on tasks.

Indeed, it seems that Timothy's deep love and concern for Paul's churches was more important to the apostle than the young man's lack of confidence. Luke tells us that during his time in Ephesus, Paul also sent Timothy to Macedonia (Acts 19:22). Many think this is the trip Paul refers to in his letter to the Philippians. And in his words to the church there Paul talks of

Timothy's remarkable pastoral heart. He writes, "I hope in the Lord Jesus to send Timothy to you soon, so that I may be cheered by news of you. I have no one like him who will be genuinely concerned for your welfare". Paul may have sent Timothy to Macedonia to encourage the congregations there to give money for a collection Paul was organising to help those of the church in Jerusalem who were poor. It was a big project for Paul and one he was keen to ensure was successful, not just to help those in need but to show the Jerusalem church that his Gentile believers were in unity with them, their Jewish Christian brethren. By sending Timothy ahead, Paul was probably hoping to avoid the embarrassing scenario of arriving in Macedonia and Achaia only to find that the believers had not collected enough money.

L uke tells us that Timothy accompanied Paul to Jerusalem along with delegates from the Gentile churches that Paul had founded. They probably accompanied him to present the offerings their congregations had gathered.[260] We are told that Paul "was accompanied by Sopater son of Pyrrhus from Beroea, by Aristarchus and Secundus from Thessalonica, by Gaius from Derbe, and by Timothy, as well as by Tychicus and Trophimus from Asia" (Acts 20:4). However, despite Paul's good intentions, this trip did not go well. Paul was a controversial character in Jerusalem and false rumours had been circulating that he had been encouraging Jewish parents not to circumcise their children or follow the Law of Moses (21:20-21). Erroneous claims were also made that he had brought one of the Gentile delegates from Ephesus, Trophimus, into the Temple, an act that carried the death sentence (verses 27-29).

Paul ended up under house arrest in Rome and Timothy was with him during at least some of this difficult time, as most of the letters written during Paul's captivity have Timothy credited as co-author. That he remained with his mentor after his arrest illustrates the extent of Timothy's faithfulness, a characteristic that was highly valued by Paul. His involvement in Paul's letter writing is, for instance, reflected in the start of the letter to the Philippians which begins: "Paul and Timothy, servants of Christ Jesus, to all the saints in Christ Jesus who are in Philippi". The letters to the Colossians and Philemon, which are also believed to have been written about this time, open by stating that they are from both Paul and Timothy. How highly Paul valued Timothy's company is reflected in his words to the Philippian church in which he wrote that he would send Timothy to them "as soon as I see how things go with me", which may well mean once he had found out whether he was going to be freed from his house arrest (Philippians 2:23b). This implies that Paul did not want to be parted from Timothy while he was in captivity.

These are not the only letters that Paul says are from Timothy. His name appears alongside Paul's in 2 Corinthians, 1 Thessalonians and 2 Thessalonians as well. It is often thought that Paul credits him in this way simply because Timothy was known to most of these churches or that he acted as a type of secretary or amanuensis, helping Paul write down his thoughts. However, he may well have been more involved in the actual composition of some of these letters. The letter to the Colossians is often cited as the one Timothy is likely to have had a particularly key role in writing, as it differs in style and language from others written by Paul. Perhaps Paul asked Timothy to present his thoughts in a way that were more accessible to the Colossians, as Timothy came from a similar area and had a similar background to them.[261]

Scholars debate what happened to Paul after his house arrest, but evidence in the Pastorals (1 and 2 Timothy and Titus) implies that Paul was released and continued his missionary work for a period of time, while 1 and 2 Timothy show that at some point after his release from house arrest in Rome Paul gave Timothy the task of tackling problems in the church at Ephesus. Paul wrote to Timothy saying:

> *I urge you, as I did when I was on my way to Macedonia, to remain in Ephesus so that you may instruct certain people not to teach any different doctrine, and not to occupy themselves with myths and endless genealogies that promote speculations rather than divine training that is known by faith. (I Timothy 1:3-4)*

This would have been a big challenge. These verses reflect that there were major problems with false teaching in the church, which appear to have involved the misuse of some of the material in the book of Genesis and possibly peddling a belief that salvation was limited to those who possessed certain secretive knowledge.[262] Timothy's role was to put an end to this false teaching and replace leaders who refused to change their ways.

This was another difficult task on a par with the challenge Timothy had faced at Corinth, and Paul clearly hoped his protégé had by this point gained more confidence. However, there are clear signs that Timothy was struggling and that Paul was worried about him. The letters 1 and 2 Timothy are addressed to Timothy himself and through them we gain an insight into the concerns Paul had about his spiritual son. It appears Timothy was lacking confidence and was backing away from carrying out his role as Paul had hoped. Paul encouraged him that he was called and equipped for the task. He exhorts Timothy not to "neglect the gift that is in you, which was given to you through prophecy and the laying on of hands" (1 Timothy 4:14). Similarly, he appeals to him to "rekindle the gift of God that is within you through the laying on of my hands" and also tells him to "do the work of an evangelist" and carry out his "ministry fully" (2 Timothy 1:6; 4:5b). Paul would only need to exhort and encourage Timothy if he felt he was falling short in some way.

So, what may have been holding Timothy back? He is often accused of being timid because Paul writes to him in 2 Timothy (1:7), saying, "God did not give us a spirit of cowardice, but rather a spirit of power and of love and of self-discipline". Clearly, Timothy was struggling with fear and this appears to have made him afraid to speak out publicly for Christ in Ephesus.²⁶³ This is also reflected in words Paul wrote to Timothy (1:8a), exhorting him to not "be ashamed, then, of the testimony about our Lord or of me his prisoner". However, Timothy's fears need to be put in context. By the time Paul wrote these things he had been imprisoned again, but this time expected his confinement to end in execution (4:6-8). This letter probably fits a date of around AD 65, when Emperor Nero had begun his terrifying persecution of Christians.²⁶⁴ No wonder Timothy was afraid. How many of us would not feel the same way if we knew that publicly standing up for our faith could lead to our deaths?

Paul writes from prison that he recalls Timothy's tears (2 Timothy 1:4a). If this refers, as some commentators suggest, to Paul's arrest, this implies that Timothy watched his spiritual father being dragged away to prison.²⁶⁵ Such trauma must have affected him and is likely to have made him nervous about proclaiming his faith.

This explains the many references in 2 Timothy to suffering and persecution. Paul encourages Timothy to "share in suffering like a good soldier of Christ Jesus" (2:3). He tells him to "proclaim the message; be persistent whether the time is favourable or unfavourable" (4:2a). Paul also reminds Timothy of the suffering he witnessed him endure when they worked together and offers him the chilling words that "all who want to live a godly life in Christ Jesus will be persecuted" (3:10-12). Paul was clearly worried about his protégé and whether he would have the courage to follow in his footsteps because the path he was asking him to pursue was so very difficult. His fears may have been particularly intense because it is possible he saw Timothy as his successor and with his own death imminent it was essential that Timothy rose to the challenge and had the courage to continue Paul's work and pass on his teaching.[266]

On top of all this, Timothy had health issues that such stress was unlikely to help. Paul advised him to, "no longer drink only water, but take a little wine for the sake of your stomach and your frequent ailments" (1 Timothy 5:23). Timothy may have been abstaining from wine because some of the elders in Ephesus drank too much and he wanted to set a good example of how to behave as a leader.[267] However, Paul clearly thought that some wine taken for medicinal purposes would help with his health issues. Wine was often used to treat indigestion, so it may have been this or something similar.[268] Timothy's physical weakness reminds us that even Christians who worked alongside Paul were not all healed of their ailments and continued to serve God while struggling with imperfect health.

We do not know whether Timothy managed to gain the courage to fulfil his calling as Paul hoped. However, there is a verse in the book of Hebrews that may suggest he did. We are unsure when the letter to the Hebrews was written, but a date in the AD 60s seems likely.[269] In this letter (13:23) the author says, "I want you to know that our brother Timothy has been set free; and if he comes in time, he will be with me when I see you". This implies that Timothy had been arrested, something that is not likely to have happened if he had been too afraid to be open about his faith. It is possible that he was arrested trying to visit Paul in prison in Rome, because Paul had asked him in his letter from his cell to do his best "to come to me soon" (2 Timothy 4:9). Paul was clearly feeling very lonely, for he talked of having no one with him apart from Luke and in such circumstances it seems likely he would have been desperate to see Timothy, his child in the faith for whom he cared for so deeply (4:10-11a). He appealed to Timothy to "do your best to come before winter" and asked him to pick up his cloak and parchments from Troas on the way (13. 21a). It is possible that Timothy was arrested fulfilling Paul's request, either en route to visiting Paul or once he'd reached Rome. Therefore, we do not know whether he got to see Paul before the apostle's execution. We can only imagine how devastated Timothy would have been if he had failed to see his spiritual father one last time before his death.

There is also legendary material which suggests that Timothy found the courage to carry on his ministry in Ephesus and stand up for his faith. This says Timothy continued working in Ephesus in the years following Paul's death and was clubbed and stoned to death in AD 97, when he tried to stop a pagan ceremony.[270]

Timothy has often been unfairly branded nervous and timid. However, that is to fail to appreciate the dangerous circumstances in which he worked, where speaking out for Christ could lead to being reviled, physically abused and even killed. Indeed, for Timothy to accompany Paul on his missionary journeys at such a young age, knowing full well how Paul himself had suffered, shows real bravery. He did not always succeed and he struggled to find the courage to fulfil his calling, but that is the reality for all of us – none of us is without fear and weakness that make it hard to do God's will. Indeed, Timothy is an encouragement to us all, that despite his struggles, he made a difference. He was a real support to Paul, playing an important role in the composition of his letters and showing God's love to the churches he and Paul had founded. He also reminds us how much the Church misses out if it "despises" younger people and fails to recognise the gifts that are bestowed upon them to enable them to carry out God's work.

Ａnd, as Paul reminded Timothy when talking about his commissioning through the laying on of hands, we serve God not through our own strength or because we never get things wrong but because God calls and equips us by his Spirit. Timothy's story is, then, an encouragement to us all.

Endnotes

[1] William Barclay, *The Gospel of Luke* (Edinburgh: St Andrew Press, 1967), 61.

[2] Joachim Jeremias, *Jerusalem in the Time of Jesus* (London: SCM, 1969), 311.

[3] Barclay, *The Gospel of Luke*, 61.

[4] Michael Card, *Luke: the Gospel of amazement* (Downers Grove, IL: InterVarsity Press, 2011), 212.

[5] Craig L. Blomberg, *Contagious Holiness* (Downers Grove, IL: InterVarsity Press, 2005), 103.

[6] Ben Witherington III, *Women and the Genesis of Christianity* (Cambridge: University Press, 1990), 100.

[7] Witherington, *Women and the Genesis of Christianity*, 100.

[8] Mary Stromer Hanson, *The New Perspective on Mary and Martha* (Eugene, OR: Wipf & Stock, 2013), 36-37.

[9] Raymond E. Brown, *The Gospel According to John 1-XII* (New York: Macmillan, 1975), 454.

[10] Richard Bauckham, *Jesus and the Eyewitnesses* (Grand Rapids, MI: William B. Eerdmans, 2006), 190-194.

[11] Elisabeth Schüssler Fiorenza, *In Memory of Her* (New York: Crossroad, 2002), 128.

[12] Iacobius de Voragine, "Of Mary Magdalene", *The Golden Legend*, volume 4. www.intratext.com/ixt/ENG1293/_P4Y.HTM, accessed 4 February 2020.

[13] A. Butler, *Lives of the Saints*, volume 7 (Collegeville, Minnesota: Burns & Oates, 2000), 236.

[14] Witherington, *Women and the Genesis of Christianity*, 99.

[15] See William Barclay's commentary on Matthew 23 at: www.studylight.org/commentaries/dsb/matthew-23.html, accessed 4 February 2020.

[16] Jeremias, *Jerusalem in the Time of Jesus*, 251.

[17] Barclay, *The Gospel of Luke*, 161.

[18] Leon Morris, *Luke* (London: InterVarsity Press, 1974), 223.

[19] D. A. Carson, *The Gospel According to John* (Grand Rapids, MI: Willian B. Eerdmans, 1991), 189.

[20] A. M. Hunter, *The Gospel According to John* (Cambridge: University Press, 1993), 85.

[21] Jeremias, *Jerusalem in the Time of Jesus*, 235-236, 253-254.

[22] W. L. Lane, *The Gospel of Mark* (Grand Rapids, MI: W. B. Eerdmans, 1974), 439-440.

[23] See the discussion in W. L. Chandler, *The Trial of Jesus from a Lawyer's Standpoint*, volume 1 (New York: Federal Book Company, 1925), 284-286, 363-365.

[24] John Wenham, *The Easter Enigma* (Exeter: Paternoster Press, 1984), 67.

[25] See, for example, M. de Jonge, "Nicodemus and Jesus: some observations on misunderstanding and understanding in the fourth Gospel", *Bulletin of the John Rylands Library*, 1971, 53(2): 337-359.

[26] A. Butler, *The Lives of the Primitive Fathers, Martyrs, and Other Principal Saints, volume 8* (Edinburgh: J. Moir, 1799), 41-43, 51-52.

[27] Bauckham, *The Testimony of the Beloved Disciple* (Grand Rapids, MI: Baker Academic, 2007), 137-172.

[28] Esther A. de Boer, "The Lukan Mary Magdalene and the Other Women Following Jesus", in Amy-Jill Levine (ed.), *A Feminist Companion to Luke* (Cleveland, Ohio: Pilgrim Press, 2001), 144.

[29] Richard Bauckham, *Gospel Women* (London: T & T Clark, 2002), 112.

[30] Bauckham, *Gospel Women*, 121-135.

[31] Barbara E. Reid, *Choosing the Better Part* (Collegeville, Minnesota: Liturgical Press, 1996), 127.

[32] Witherington, *Women and the Genesis of Christianity*, 110.

[33] Bauckham, *Gospel Women*, 119-120, 134-135.

[34] Bauckham, *Gospel Women*, 135-137, 141, 150-158.

[35] Bauckham, *Gospel Women*, 142, 145-146.

[36] Turid Karlsen Seim, *The Double Message* (London: T & T Clark, 1990), 36.

[37] Barclay, *The Gospel of Luke*, 305.

[38] Bauckham, *Gospel Women*, 270.

[39] Origen, *Contra Celsum*, 2:55. Translation found at: www.newadvent.org/fathers/04162.htm, accessed 4 February 2020.

[40] Bauckham, *Gospel Women*, 182, 184, 186.

[41] Thomas R. Schreiner, *Romans* (Grand Rapids, MI: Baker Academic, 1998), 796.

[42] Rena Pederson, *The Lost Apostle* (San Francisco, CA: Jossey-Bass, 2006), 165-166. Pederson says that this is why the translators of the NRSV Bible decided to change the name in Romans 16:7 to the female, Junia, in 1989, a decision which influenced other Bible translations to follow suit.

[43] For example: "they are well known to the apostles" (New English Translation), and "they are noteworthy in the eyes of the apostles" (Christian Standard Bible).

[44] Schreiner, *Romans*, 796.

45 Quoted in Bernadette Brooten, "Junia, Outstanding among the Apostles (Romans 16:7)", in Arlene Swidler and Leonard Swidler (eds), *Women Priests: a Catholic commentary on the Vatican declaration* (New York: Paulist Press, 1977), 141.
46 Bauckham, *Gospel Women*, 170, 181.
47 Brooten, "Junia, Outstanding among the Apostles", 143.
48 Bauckham, *Gospel Women*, 198.
49 James Dunn, *Jesus, Paul and the Gospels* (Grand Rapids, MI: William B. Eerdmans: 2011), 174.
50 Pederson, *The Lost Apostle*, 190-191.
51 Pederson, *The Lost Apostle*, 190.
52 I have used the dates given by Geza Vermes in *The True Herod* (London: Bloomsbury, 2014) for all the Herodian rulers.
53 N. Gelb, *Herod the Great: statesman, visionary, tyrant* (Plymouth: Rowman, 2013), xii.
54 M. C. Tenney, *New Testament Times* (London: InterVarsity Press, 1965), 66.
55 Vermes, *The True Herod*, 46.
56 F. F. Bruce, *New Testament History* (New York: Doubleday, 1980), 22.
57 Vermes, *The True Herod*, 99.
58 Alan Storkey, *Jesus and Politics: confronting the powers* (Grand Rapids, MI: Baker Academic, 2005), 21.
59 Flavius Josephus, "The Antiquities of the Jews", in William Whiston (ed.), *Josephus: the complete works* (Nashville, TN: Thomas Nelson, 1998), 17.191.
60 J. Rogerson, *Atlas of the Bible* (London: Macdonald, 1985), 82.
61 Vermes, *The True Herod*, 79.
62 William Barclay, *The Gospel of Mark* (Edinburgh: St Andrew Press, 1973), 322.
63 Storkey, *Jesus and Politics*, 18.
64 Rogerson, *Atlas of the Bible*, 211.
65 Josephus, "The Antiquities of the Jews", 18.106.
66 William Barclay, *The Gospel of Matthew*. www.studylight.org/commentaries/dsb/matthew-14.html, accessed 14 April 2020.
67 Bruce, *New Testament History*, 28.
68 Barclay, *The Gospel of Mark*, 150.
69 Storkey, *Jesus and Politics*, 86.
70 Gerhard A. Krodel, *Acts* (Minneapolis, MN: Augsburg, 1986), 227.
71 Vermes, *The True Herod*, 130.
72 Vermes, *The True Herod*, 133.
73 Vermes, *The True Herod*, 134.
74 Krodel, *Acts*, 217-218.
75 Bruce, *New Testament History*, 263.
76 Bruce, *New Testament History*, 344.
77 Vermes, *The True Herod*, 139.
78 Vermes, *The True Herod*, 141-143.
79 "Iulius Agrippa", in Simon Hornblower (ed.), *The Oxford Classical Dictionary* (Oxford: OUP, 2012), 756.
80 Vermes, *The True Herod*, 141.
81 Bruce, *New Testament History*, 391.
82 James R. Edwards, *The Gospel According to Luke* (Grand Rapids, MI: William B. Eerdmans, 2015), talks of Anna as "a requisite second witness", 88.
83 Witherington, *Women and the Genesis of Christianity*, 209.
84 Barbara Reid, *Choosing the Better Part? Women in the Gospel of Luke* (Collegeville, MN: Liturgical Press), 1996, 93.
85 Richard Bauckham, *Gospel Women*, 99.
86 Raymond E. Brown, *The Birth of the Messiah* (London: Geoffrey Chapman, 1978), 467, note 66.
87 F. F. Bruce, *The Acts of the Apostles* (London: Tyndale Press, 1951), 103. The first disciples appear to have continued to attend these Temple services, for Acts 3:1 records Peter and John "going up to the temple at the hour of prayer, at three o'clock in the afternoon."
88 "Sacrifice and Temple Service", in Craig A. Evans and Stanley Porter (eds), *Dictionary of New Testament Background* (Downers Grove, IL: InterVarsity Press, 2000), 1041, 1044.
89 John Rogerson (ed.), *Beginning Old Testament Study* (London: SPCK, 1983), 67-68.
90 Emil Schürer, *The History of the Jewish People in the Age of Jesus Christ* (Edinburgh: T & T Clark, 1979), 303, 307.
91 Dr J. Randall Price, *Rose Guide to the Temple* (Torrance, CA: Rose, 2012), 81.

[92] Article on "Sacrifice and Temple Service", in Evans and Porter (eds), *Dictionary of New Testament Background*, 1038-1039, 1046.

[93] Price, *Rose Guide to the Temple*, 80.

[94] Mishnah Sukkah 5:2, 5:3. www.sefaria.org/Mishnah_Sukkah.5.2?lang=bi, and www.chabad.org/library/article_cdo/aid/4491/jewish/The-Drawing-of-the-Water.htm, accessed 18 July 2022.

[95] Alec Garrard, *The Splendour of the Temple* (Grand Rapids, MI: Kregel, 2000), 64. This is reflected in Mark 1:40-45, where Jesus instructs a leper he has healed to show himself to the priest in accordance with Jewish Law. After the priest confirmed his healing, the man would have to go to the Temple and bathe in the Chamber of the Leper.

[96] "Fasting", in Joel B. Green et al. (eds), *Dictionary of Jesus and the Gospels* (Leicester: InterVarsity Press, 1992), 233.

[97] "Prophets, Prophecy", in Green et al. (eds), *Dictionary of Jesus and the Gospels*, 637.

[98] Brown, *The Birth of the Messiah*, 442.

[99] Bruce, *New Testament History* (p. 133), says this was the predominant belief about the messiah in Jesus' day.

[100] "Kingdom of God/Kingdom of Heaven", in Green et al. (eds), *Dictionary of Jesus and the Gospels*, 418.

[101] John Drane, *Introducing the New Testament* (Oxford: Lion, 1999), 112.

[102] Bauckham, *Gospel Women*, 77.

[103] Bauckham, *Gospel Women*, 88-98.

[104] Edwards, in *The Gospel According to Luke* (p. 88), says that as a representative of one of the lost tribes of Israel Anna might represent "the lost" Jesus came to restore.

[105] Edwards, *The Gospel According to Luke*, 88.

[106] Ben Witherington III, "Mary, Simeon or Anna: who first recognised Jesus as Messiah?" www.biblicalarchaeology.org/daily/biblical-topics/new-testament/mary-simeon-or-anna-who-first-recognized-jesus-as-messiah, accessed 14 April 2020.

[107] See R. J. Coggins, *Samaritans and Jews* (Oxford: Blackwell, 1975), 10.

[108] "Samaritans", in Green et al. (eds), *Dictionary of Jesus and the Gospels*, 726.

[109] Coggins, *Samaritans and Jews*, 17-18.

[110] "Samaritans", in Green et al. (eds), *Dictionary of Jesus and the Gospels*, 726.

[111] Carson, *The Gospel According to John*, 222.

[112] Alan D. Crown, *The Samaritans* (Tübingen: JCB Mohr, 1989), 18.

[113] Jeremias, *Jerusalem in the Time of Jesus*, 356.

[114] William Barclay, *The Gospel of John*, volume 1 (Philadelphia, PA: Westminster Press, 1975), 147.

[115] Josephus, "The Antiquities of the Jews", 20.118.

[116] This is reflected in the words the woman at the well said to Jesus: "I know that Messiah is coming' (who is called Christ). 'When he comes, he will proclaim all things to us" (John 4:25).

[117] Ben Witherington III, *The Acts of the Apostles* (Grand Rapids, MI: William B. Eerdmans, 1998), 289.

[118] Bruce, *New Testament History*, 229.

[119] Barclay, *The Gospel of John*, volume 1, 151.

[120] C. K. Barrett, *The Gospel According to St John* (London: SPCK, 1978), 240.

[121] Bauckham, *Jesus and the Eyewitnesses*, 387.

[122] Revd Alban Butler, *Butler's Lives of the Saints*, https://archive.org/stream/ButlersLivesOfTheSaintsCompleteEdition/ButlersLivesOfTheSaintsCompleteEdition_djvu.txt, 636, accessed 14 April 2020.

[123] Vincent J. Pastro, *Enflamed by the Sacramental Word* (Eugene, OR: Pickwick, 2010), 105.

[124] Davide Lerner and Esra Whitehouse (10 May 2018), "Not Muslim, Not Jewish: ancient community in the West Bank feels increasingly Israeli". www.haaretz.com/israel-news/.premium.MAGAZINE-for-ancient-samaritan-community-a-new-test-of-loyalty-1.6075509, accessed 14 April 2020.

[125] G. Russell, *Heirs to the Forgotten Kingdom* (London: Simon & Schuster, 2015), 176.

[126] Helena Merriman, "The Modern Trials of the Ancient Samaritans" (3 January 2011), BBC News website. www.bbc.co.uk/news/world-middle-east-12069728, accessed 14 April 2020.

[127] Hershel Shanks and Ben Witherington III, *The Brother of Jesus* (London: Continuum, 2003), 103-105.

[128] Peter Davids gives the dates of around AD 40-62 as those traditionally given for James presiding over the Jerusalem church. See Peter H. Davids, *The Epistle of James* (Exeter: Paternoster Press, 1982), 2.

[129] Bruce, *New Testament History*, 371.

[130] See Ronald Y. K. Fung, *The Epistle to the Galatians* (Grand Rapids, MI: William B. Eerdmans, 1988), 78.

[131] Shanks and Witherington, *The Brother of Jesus*, 114.

[132] Krodel, *Acts*, 284.

[133] William Hendriksen, *Galatians* (Edinburgh: Banner of Truth, 1974), 90.

[134] Bruce, *New Testament History*, 288.

Endnotes

135 *Recognitions of Clement*, Book 1, Chapter LXX.
136 Shanks and Witherington, *The Brother of Jesus*, 128.
137 Shanks and Witherington, *The Brother of Jesus*, 166.
138 Krodel, *Acts*, 404.
139 Eusebius, *Ecclesiastical History*, II.23.6.
140 Bruce, *New Testament History*, 348.
141 Shanks and Witherington, *The Brother of Jesus*, 93.
142 Ralph P. Martin, *James* (Dallas, TX: Word Books, 1988), lxi.
143 Bernd Kollmann, *Joseph Barnabas: his life and legacy* (Collegeville, MN: Liturgical Press, 2004), 7-8.
144 Kollmann, *Joseph Barnabas*, 10.
145 Bruce, *The Acts of the Apostles*, 278.
146 Kollmann, *Joseph Barnabas*, 58.
147 Bruce, *New Testament History*, 206, 243.
148 I. Howard Marshall, *Acts* (Leicester: InterVarsity Press, 1980), 198.
149 Marshall, *Acts*, 202.
150 Bruce, *The Acts of the Apostles*, 236.
151 Krodel, *Acts*, 210.
152 Note there are textual issues with this verse, although many believe it makes sense to understand that they returned "from" rather than "to" Jerusalem.
153 Bruce, *New Testament History*, 278.
154 M. C. Tenney, *New Testament Times* (London: Inter-Varsity Press, 1965), 230.
155 Tenney, *New Testament Times*, 235.
156 Richard Bauckham, "Barnabas in Galatians", *Journal for the Study of the New Testament*, 2, 1979, 62-64. We cannot be certain that the Letter to the Galatians was written to the churches Barnabas and Paul founded in South Galatia rather than churches in North Galatia, but this is the opinion of many scholars including Bauckham.
157 See Acts 15. I take the position that the Council of Jerusalem took place after the Antioch incident recorded in Galatians 2:11-14. However, this is a hotly debated subject.
158 Bauckham, Barnabas in Galatians, 67.
159 Philip Edgcumbe Hughes, *A Commentary on the Epistle to the Hebrews* (Grand Rapids, MI: William B. Eerdmans, 1990), 24-25.
160 Kollmann, *Joseph Barnabas*, 47.
161 Marshall, *Acts*, 126. In other contexts, such as Acts 11:20 it is used to mean Greek-speaking Gentiles.
162 Witherington, *The Acts of the Apostles*, 248.
163 James D. G. Dunn, *The Acts of the Apostles* (Peterborough: Epworth Press, 1996), 86.
164 Marshall, *Acts*, 125-126.
165 Ben F. Meyer, *The Early Christians* (Eugene, OR: Wipf & Stock, 1986), 68.
166 The Greek of this verse is unclear. It could describe one synagogue of the Freedmen that included all these nationalities or several synagogues which served each of the nationalities listed. Ben Witherington, *The Acts of the Apostles*, says the one synagogue interpretation is the most straightforward (p. 253).
167 Witherington, *The Acts of the Apostles*, 249. The Greek of Acts 6:1 does not include the word food, however, even though many translations have it.
168 Meyer, *The Early Christians*, 68.
169 Witherington, *The Acts of the Apostles*, 248.
170 Witherington, *The Acts of the Apostles*, 248, quotes from C. Keener, Bible Background Commentary (Downers Grove: InterVarsity, 1993), 338.
171 "Temple, Jewish" in Evans and Porter (eds), *Dictionary of New Testament Background*, 1171.
172 Drane, *Introducing the New Testament*, 248.
173 W. D. Davies, *The Gospel of the Land* (Sheffield: JSOT Press, 1994), 267-272.
174 For example, Dunn, *The Acts of the Apostles*, 96.
175 W. D. Davies, *The Gospel of the Land*, says the "static edifice" of the Temple was "misguided" but the "movable tent" followed the "divine pattern" (p. 271).
176 Philip Francis Esler, *Commentary and Gospel in Luke-Acts* (Cambridge: University Press, 1987), 149.
177 Esler, *Commentary and Gospel in Luke-Acts*, 151-152, 156.
178 Severus, Chronicle ii,30.6, quoted in Bruce, *New Testament History*, 383.
179 Tertullian, "*Apology*", 50, in Rev. C. Dodgson (trans.), *Apologetic and Practical Treatises* (Oxford: John Henry Parker, 1842).
180 Robert C. Tannehill, *The Narrative Unity of Luke-Acts*, volume 2 (Minneapolis, MN: Fortress Press, 1990), 100.

[181] Witherington, *The Acts of the Apostles*, 277.

[182] Butler, "The Invention of St Stephen", in *The Lives of the Saints*, volume 8 (Edinburgh: J. Moir, 1799), 41.

[183] William Hendriksen, *Mark* (Edinburgh: Banner of Truth, 1975), 3.

[184] There is disagreement about how to read this text, but in the context, it makes more sense if Barnabas and Saul are returning *from* Jerusalem rather than returning to it as the alternative reading suggests.

[185] Witherington, *The Acts of the Apostles*, 396.

[186] Krodel, *Acts*, 231.

[187] F. F. Bruce, *The Epistles to the Colossians, to Philemon and to the Ephesians* (Grand Rapids, MI: William B. Eerdmans, 1984), 179.

[188] I am taking the traditional position that Paul wrote 1 and 2 Timothy, although many scholars debate this. For the arguments in support of Pauline authorship see the article on "Timothy and Titus, Epistles to", in J. D. Douglas (ed.), *The Illustrated Bible Dictionary*, part 3 (Leicester: InterVarsity Press, 1980), 1570-1571.

[189] R. Alan Cole, *Mark* (Leicester: InterVarsity Press, 1989), 35-36.

[190] Bauckham, *Jesus and the Eyewitnesses*, 206-207.

[191] George Edmundson, *The Church in Rome in the First Century* (New York: Longmans, Green & Co., 1913), 14, 27-29, 50-51, 56-58.

[192] Ben Witherington III, *The Gospel of Mark: a socio-rhetorical commentary* (Grand Rapids, MI: William B. Eerdmans, 2001), 24-26. Witherington gives Mark 10:45, the presentation of the Last Supper and the themes of suffering and servanthood as examples of the similarities between Mark's Gospel and Paul and Peter's work.

[193] Bauckham, *Jesus and the Eyewitnesses*, 161.

[194] C. E. B. Cranfield, *The Gospel According to St Mark* (Cambridge: University Press, 1974), 20.

[195] Cole, *Mark*, 37-39.

[196] Bruce, *New Testament History*, 399-401.

[197] Hendriksen, *Mark*, 601-602.

[198] Cranfield, *The Gospel According to St Mark*, 438-439.

[199] Bruce, *The Acts of the Apostles*, 247.

[200] Witherington, *The Acts of the Apostles*, 387.

[201] Witherington, *Conflict and Community in Corinth*, 183.

[202] Jennifer A. Glancy, *Slavery in Early Christianity* (Oxford: OUP, 2002), 74-75, 78-79, 80-85.

[203] Glancy, *Slavery in Early Christianity*, 42-43. See also "Slavery", in Evans and Porter (eds), *Dictionary of New Testament Background*, 1126.

[204] *The Letter to Philemon* (Grand Rapids, MI: William B. Eerdmans, 2000), 15-16.

[205] Glancy, *Slavery in Early Christianity*, 9.

[206] G. B. Caird, *Paul's Letters from Prison* (Oxford: OUP, 1976), 214.

[207] James Albert Harrill, *Slaves in the New Testament* (Minneapolis, MN: Fortress Press, 2006), 6.

[208] Markus Barth and Helmut Blanke, *The Letter to Philemon*, 16, 30.

[209] Ben Witherington III, *The Letters to Philemon, the Colossians, and the Ephesians* (Grand Rapids, MI: William B. Eerdmans, 2007), 29.

[210] Witherington, *Conflict and Community in Corinth*, 183.

[211] Harold H. Hoehner, *Ephesians* (Grand Rapids, MI: Baker Academic, 2002), 802.

[212] *The Letter to Philemon*, 52-53.

[213] Hendrik Mouritsen, *The Freedman in the Roman World* (Cambridge: University Press, 2011), 36.

[214] Quoted in Jim Hill and Rand Cheadle, *The Bible Tells Me So* (New York: Anchor Books/Doubleday, 1996), 6.

[215] Solomon Northup, *Twelve Years a Slave* (New York: Miller, Orton & Mulligan, 1855), 127-128.

[216] Quoted in Cheadle, *The Bible Tells Me So*, 5.

[217] F. F. Bruce, *Paul: apostle of the free spirit* (Carlisle: Paternoster Press, 1992), 401.

[218] Harriet Beecher Stowe, *Uncle Tom's Cabin* (London: John Cassell, 1852), x.

[219] Bruce, *Paul*, 406.

[220] Witherington, *The Acts of the Apostles*, 56.

[221] Bruce, *The Acts of the Apostles*, 5-6.

[222] Bruce, *New Testament History*, 360.

[223] John Philips, *Exploring the Pastorals* (Grand Rapids, MI: Kregel, 2004), 447.

[224] See Witherington, *The Acts of the Apostles*, 54.

[225] Richard N. Longenecker, *Acts* (Grand Rapids, MI: Zondervan, 1995), 254.

[226] Witherington, *The Acts of the Apostles*, 489-490.

[227] Card, *Luke*, 17.

228 Keith F. Nickle, *The Synoptic Gospels* (Louisville, KY: John Knox Press, 2001), 141.
229 I. Howard Marshall, *Luke - Historian and Theologian* (Paternoster Press, 1970), 66.
230 "Luke, Gospel of", in Green et al. (eds), *Dictionary of Jesus and the Gospels*, 497.
231 Stuart H. Merriam, *Paul the Apostle: at the edge by faith* (Tucson, AZ: Fenestra, 2004), 248.
232 Ben Witherington III, *Letters and Homilies for Hellenized Christians* (Downers Grove, IL: InterVarsity Press, 2006), 54-62, 67-68.
233 Bruce, *Paul:* 16.
234 Ben Witherington III, *New Testament History* (Grand Rapids, MI: Baker Academic, 2001), 386-387.
235 Bruce, *The Acts of the Apostles*, 6.
236 Marshall, *Acts*, 292-293.
237 Bruce, *New Testament History*, 297-298.
238 Bruce, *The Acts of the Apostles*, 343.
239 Longenecker, *Acts*, 277.
240 Dunn, *The Acts of the Apostles*, 241-242.
241 Witherington, *The Acts of the Apostles*, 547-548.
242 Witherington, *New Testament History*, 270.
243 Wayne A. Meeks, *The First Urban Christians: the social world of Paul the Apostle* (New Haven, CT: Yale University Press, 2003), 29.
244 Lionel Casson, *Travel in the Ancient World* (London: Book Club Associates, 1979), 152-155.
245 Casson, *Travel in the Ancient World*, 121-122.
246 Witherington, *The Acts of the Apostles*, 556-558.
247 Witherington, *Letters and Homilies for Hellenized Christians*, volume 1, 220-221, 223, 226-227, 232.
248 I. Howard Marshall, *The Pastoral Epistles* (Edinburgh: T & T Clarke, 1999), 466-467. This would explain the puzzling reference to the Adam and Eve story in 1 Timothy 2:13-15.
249 N. T. Wright, *Paul for Everyone: the pastoral letters* (London: SPCK, 2003), 24-27.
250 Robert Banks, *Paul's Idea of Community* (Grand Rapids, MI: Baker Academic, 1994), 117.
251 Leon Morris, *1 Corinthians* (Leicester: InterVarsity Press, 1995), suggests thirty would be the maximum if the church was hosted in the room usually used for entertaining. However, Anthony C. Thiselton, in *1 Corinthians* (Michigan: William B. Eerdmans, 2006), suggests fifty to sixty could have been accommodated if people were standing in the atrium of houses too.
252 Witherington, *The Acts of the Apostles*, 590.
253 Thiselton, in *1 Corinthians*, attributes this thought to F. F. Bruce.
254 Lance Pierson, *In the Steps of Timothy* (Leicester: InterVarsity Press, 1995), 47.
255 Marshall, *Acts*, 260.
256 Bruce, in *Paul: apostle of the free spirit*, believes Paul arrived at Ephesus on this occasion in AD 52 and stayed there for about three years.
257 Morris, *1 Corinthians*, 81.
258 Marshall, *Pastoral Epistles*, 560.
259 Pierson, *In the Steps of Timothy*, argues that Timothy was not cut out to work alone but needed to be in a team.
260 Marshall, *Acts*, 323.
261 Witherington, *The Letters to Philemon, the Colossians, and the Ephesians*, says Lystra, where Timothy was brought up, lay just outside the Roman province of Asia where Colossae was and this, together with his Greek background from his father, may have made it easier for Timothy to write in an Asiatic style that suited the Colossians.
262 Witherington, *Letters and Homilies for Hellenized Christians*, volume 1, 192-193. See also my chapter on Priscilla for more information about the nature of some of this false teaching.
263 Marshall, *Pastoral Epistles*, 699.
264 Witherington, *Letters and Homilies for Hellenized Christians*, volume 1, suggests that 2 Timothy was written between AD 65 and 67.
265 J. N. D. Kelly, *The Pastoral Epistles* (London: Adam & Charles Black, 1976), 156.
266 Witherington, *Letters and Homilies for Hellenized Christians*, volume 1, 315.
267 Marshall, *Pastoral Epistles*, 623-624
268 Kelly, *The Pastoral Epistles*, 129.
269 For example, the article on "Hebrews, Epistle to the", in J. D. Douglas (ed.), *The Illustrated Bible Dictionary*, volume 2, suggests possible dates of before AD 64 or AD 67-68.
270 Pierson, *In the Steps of Timothy*, 204, and Alban Butler, *Lives of the Fathers, Martyrs and Principal Saints: January, February and March* (Oxford: Benediction Classic, 2011), 198.